WILLIAM STYRON

LITERATURE AND LIFE: AMERICAN WRITERS

Selected list of titles in the series:

WILLIAM STYRON

Judith Ruderman

UNGAR • NEW YORK

1987

The Ungar Publishing Company
370 Lexington Avenue
New York, N.Y. 10017

Printed in the United States of America

Library of Congress Cataloging-in-Publication Data

Ruderman, Judith, 1943–
   William Styron.

   (Literature and life series)
   Bibliography: p.
   Includes index.
   1. Styron, William, 1925–   —Criticism and
interpretation.   I. Title.   II. Series.
PS3569.T9Z88   1987   813'.54   87-5093
ISBN 0-8044-2781-X

To Lee and Marjory

Contents

Acknowledgments

My first debt of gratitude goes to William Styron, who provided access to the collection of his materials at Duke University and who answered my letters promptly and graciously. In addition, I wish to thank the staff of the Duke University Manuscript Department—Dr. Mattie Russell, Curator of Manuscripts (now retired); Robert Byrd, present Curator of Manuscripts; Ellen Gartrell; and Patricia Webb—all of whom made my research easy and pleasurable. Permission to quote from unpublished documents was generously granted by William Styron and the Duke University Manuscript Department. I also wish to express my appreciation to the Continuing Education classes in 1983 and 1985 who read and discussed with me the works of William Styron, and whose delight in studying literature increased my own.

Chronology

1925   William Styron born to Pauline and William Clark Styron, Sr., on June 11 in Newport News, Virginia.

1938 or
1939   Publishes first short story (now lost) in Morrison High School newspaper.

1939   Mother dies after Styron's sophomore year in high school.

1940   Sent by father to Christchurch School, near Urbana, Va.

1940–42 Publishes in Christchurch newspaper.

1942   Enters Davidson College, Davidson, North Carolina.

1942–43 Publishes in Davidson newspaper and literary magazine.

1943   Enlists in US Marine Corps. Joins Navy V-12 Program. Transfers to Duke University, where he studies creative writing with Professor William Blackburn.

1944   Sent to Marine Training Camp, Parris Island. Mistakenly put in venereal ward for 4$^{1}/_{2}$ months.

1944–46 Publishes stories, sketches, and reviews in Duke *Archive*.

1945   Enters officers' candidate school at Camp Lejeune, NC. Commissioned as second lieutenant at Quantico.

Becomes a guard at Naval Disciplinary Barracks on Hart's Island, NY Harbor. Discharged from military after surrender of Japanese. Short stories "Autumn" and "Long Dark Road" appear in *One and Twenty: Duke Narrative and Verse, 1924–45*.

1946   Returns to Duke University in March. During summer, travels to Trieste as assistant veterinarian on cattle boat. Attends Bread Loaf Writers' Conference, Middlebury, Vermont.

1947   Fails to qualify as Rhodes Scholar. Graduates from Duke University in May. Goes to New York City and works as editor at McGraw-Hill. Enrolls in creative writing class under Hiram Haydn at the New School for Social Research. Fired from McGraw-Hill in fall. Begins work on *Lie Down in Darkness*. Gets writer's block and returns to Durham, NC, to work on manuscript.

1948   Publishes "A Moment in Trieste" in *American Vanguard*.

1949   Moves to Brooklyn, NY (Flatbush section), boarding house.

1949–50   Works on novel at Valley Cottage, near Nyack, NY. Returns to New York City in May. Publishes "The Enormous Window" (short story) in *1950 American Vanguard*.

1951   Recalled to active duty in Marine Corps. Haydn has induction postponed. Completes *Lie Down in Darkness* in April. Reenters the Marines, Second Marine Division, Camp Lejeune, NC. Undergoes long march during summer. Discharged because of congenital cataract. Publishes *Lie Down in Darkness* in September.

1952   Meets Rose Burgunder, poet, at Johns Hopkins seminar. Wins Prix de Rome Fellowship of the American

Academy of Arts and Letters. Tours England and Denmark, lives in Paris. In June and July, writes novella about forced march. Becomes friendly with other young writers, helps them launch the *Paris Review*. Arrives in Rome in October. Renews acquaintance with Rose Burgunder.

1953   Publishes "Long March" in *discovery* in February. First *Paris Review* issued in Spring. Marries Rose Burgunder in Rome on May 4. Moves with Rose to Ravello, Italy. Works on novella (never completed) about experiences as prison guard. Begins *Set This House on Fire*.

1954   Moves to Roxbury, Connecticut, farmhouse. Works on *Set This House on Fire*.

1955   Daughter Susanna born.

1956   Publishes *The Long March*.

1957   *The Long March* included in *The Best Short Stories of World War II*.

1958   Daughter Paola born.

1959   Publishes introduction to *Best Short Stories from the Paris Review*. Completes *Set This House on Fire*. Publishes portions of the novel in *Esquire* and the *Paris Review*. Son Tom born.

1960   Publishes *Set This House on Fire* in May, on seventh wedding anniversary.

1960s   Reviews books and writes essays for the *New York Review of Books*, *Harper's*, *New York Times Book Review*, *Esquire*. Becomes active in politics and civil rights.

1962   Attends Nobel Prize function at White House. Begins *The Confessions of Nat Turner*.

1963   On Board of Directors, Inter-American Foundation of
            Arts.

1964   Is teaching fellow at Silliman College, Yale University.

1966   Daughter Alexandra born. Becomes member of the
            National Institute of Arts and Letters. Lectures in
            Egypt with Robert Penn Warren. Publishes parts of *The
            Confessions of Nat Turner* in *Partisan Review, Paris Review,
            Harper's,* and *Life* in 1966 and 1967.

1967   Publishes *The Confessions of Nat Turner* in October.

1968   Wins Pulitzer Prize for *The Confessions of Nat Turner.
            William Styron's Nat Turner: Ten Black Writers Respond,*
            ed. John Henrik Clark, is published. Is delegate to
            Democratic Convention. Receives honorary degrees
            from Duke University and Tufts University.

1969   Is witness at trial of "Chicago Seven."

1970   Wins Howells Medal for Fiction, given by American
            Academy of Arts and Letters.

1970s   Begins *The Way of the Warrior* (as yet unfinished).

1971   Publishes part of *The Way of the Warrior* called "Mar-
            riott, the Marine" in *Esquire.* Is juror for National Book
            Award for Fiction.

1972   *In the Clap Shack* presented at Yale Repertory Theatre
            on December 15. Is appointed Honorary Consultant at
            Library of Congress. Covers William Faulkner's funeral
            for *Life* magazine.

1973   Publishes *In the Clap Shack* in June. Publishes screen
            play, "Dead!", coauthored with John Phillips, in *Es-
            quire.*

1974   Begins work on *Sophie's Choice*. Travels to Poland. Pub-
         lishes "The Suicide Run," part of Marine novel, in
         American Poetry Review.

1976–77 Publishes portions of *Sophie's Choice* in *Esquire* and the
         Archive (Duke University).

1977   Participates in Moscow conference of American and
         Soviet writers.

1978   Father dies.

1979   Publishes *Sophie's Choice* on his fifty-fourth birthday.
         Book is on NY *Times* bestseller list for forty weeks.

1980   Wins American Book Award for Fiction for *Sophie's
         Choice*.

1981   Delivers commencement address at Duke University.

1982   Publishes *This Quiet Dust* in November. Presents Na-
         tional Medal for Literature to John Cheever.

1983   Is president of jury, Cannes Film Festival. Film *Sophie's
         Choice* released by Universal Pictures.

1985   Publishes "Love Day," part of marine novel, in *Esquire*.

1986   Is hospitalized for depression; restructures and contin-
         ues work on *The Way of the Warrior*.

1

Revolutionary Works in an Ordinary Life

Be regular and orderly in your life like a bourgeois, so that you may be violent and original in your work.

—Quotation from Flaubert,
in William Styron's study

For an American born in the South in the era before World War II, the historical sense is as sharp and as pungent as the smell of pork barbecuing overnight on hickory chips. William Clark Styron, Jr.—a Southerner and, even more, a Virginian—has always found a consciousness of history to be his unshakable companion and a stimulus for his fiction.

Styron's roots go deep into southern soil.[1] His paternal ancestors settled in Virginia as early as 1635. His mother's people arrived there a century later and eventually produced Thomas "Stonewall" Jackson, the Confederate general who commanded at Bull Run and Chancellorsville, and who ranks as one of the most skillful tacticians in military history. As Styron looks back on his youth he sees every event intersecting with moments of historical importance. The hospital room in which he was born overlooked the spot on the James River where the *Monitor* had battled the *Merrimac* during the Civil War. No sensitive boy growing up near that river could fail to be struck by its significance as the entry point for the first explorers on the continent and, later, for the first slave ships. Civil War battlegrounds formed the physical and psychological landscape of Styron's childhood. He penned his compositions in a book that bore on its cover an engraved image of Robert E. Lee, and studied the benefits of slavery in a compulsory grammar school course in

1

Virginia history. More immediately, his paternal grandfather limped from a knee wound suffered at Chancellorsville. But Styron's preoccupation with the issue of slavery, and his sense of connection with the old South, no doubt stems in greatest part from his paternal grandmother Clark: born on a plantation in North Carolina, she had owned slaves, and in her eighties she often regaled young Billy with stories about how she cared for them and knitted them socks. Such domestic and personal incidents formed and nourished William Styron's consciousness of history.

Styron was raised in Hilton Village, then a semirural community of a few hundred people several miles up the James River from Newport News. He attended segregated schools and grew up with black servants in the home; mostly he lived at the edge of another society without having any meaningful contact with it. Yet it was to a black college not far away—the Hampton Institute—that Styron was taken for concerts and lectures by his liberal and enlightened father.

William Clark Styron, Sr., was a native North Carolinian and graduate of North Carolina College of Agriculture and Mechanical Arts (now North Carolina State University); he worked for forty years as an engineer at the Newport News Shipbuilding and Dry Dock Company. Styron's mother, Pauline Abraham, a Pennsylvanian, had met her future husband while directing the YWCA hostess house in Newport News during World War I. An accomplished musician, she studied piano and voice in Vienna as a teenager and, later, public school music instruction at the University of Pittsburgh, before becoming the music supervisor of schools in Pennsylvania and Colorado.

Soon after the birth of her son, Mrs. Styron developed cancer, underwent a series of operations, and became an invalid. Over the eleven years in which she remained housebound, she devoted herself to her only child and instilled in him her own love of music and books. Although the one musical instrument young Bill played was the harmonica—and then only briefly—he retained a belief in the vital importance of music for a fulfilled life. He also showed a very early interest in reading, an almost obsessive love of words, and a fertile imagination. An analysis of his handwriting when he was about ten revealed to his proud parents "a very natural sort of boy, bright, even witty at times, able to mimic others, and embellish a story by exaggeration, in order to make it more interesting."[2]

William Styron was fourteen and approaching his junior year in the local public high school the summer his mother died. He had been active in school affairs at Morrison High, managing the football team and serving as president of the sophomore class. But his teachers felt that he was not applying himself, and his father found him lacking in discipline. So he was sent off to an Episcopal preparatory school called Christchurch, on the banks of the Rappahannock River in Virginia near Urbana. At this small (approximately fifty) all-boys school Styron enjoyed the sense of being in an extended, close-knit family. Here he wrote for the school newspaper and yearbook, played basketball and sailed, attended chapel every day and church on Sunday— but he also took to drinking. It was during his second year at the school, when off on a beer-drinking joy ride with a classmate and two town girls, that Styron heard the news about Pearl Harbor. He did not then realize that at that moment his life was irrevocably changed; this carefree school-boy existence of an entire generation was soon to fall casualty to war.

Styron went to Christchurch an extra year, in order to graduate at seventeen (he had skipped a year in grammar school, was small for his age, and had some catching up to do). His entry on the flyleaf of his school edition of *Hamlet* records his impatience with this protracted educational experience: "Styron, W. C. II, Newport News, Virginia, Christchurch School, 1940–41–42. No more—thank the Lord." His father, ever the watchdog, thought the University of Virginia too wild a place for the likes of Bill and chose for him Hampden-Sydney College. Turned down by that school because of his indifferent record at Christchurch, he was sent to another sober and respectable Presbyterian institution: Davidson College near Charlotte, North Carolina. Styron joined a fraternity and took up his favorite activities, writing features for the college newspaper and serving on the editorial staff of the literary magazine. He also set about losing his Tidewater accent after being ribbed by "cornpone southerners." Styron felt bound in by the sanctimonious atmosphere at Davidson; in addition, the ever-present specter of war precluded close ties to the college. So at age eighteen Styron joined the Navy V-12 program, thinking how glamorous and manly it would be to serve as a marine officer. With some sense of release he was transferred by order of the United States government to Duke University in the tobacco town of Durham.

Duke had a reputation among Tidewater Virginians as a country-club university for wealthy and intellectually benighted Northerners. Here Styron attended regular classes but wore a uniform and submitted to a quasi-military discipline. He found the atmosphere at Duke in 1943 as aggressively militaristic as Davidson's. It was also equally puritanical: the Duke coeds wore white gloves on off-campus dates, symbolic of the purity of the 1940s—a rotten time for romance, as Styron would later characterize it. For relief Styron read André Gide during physics class and was nearly expelled and shipped to the Pacific because of it. His grades were average to poor: later, his four-time flunking of physics would prevent his receiving a Rhodes scholarship. In late 1944, with an undistinguished college record, Styron went off to active duty.

In the Parris Island marine boot camp, a week after his arrival as a tender and inexperienced nineteen-year-old, Styron was mistakenly diagnosed as having syphilis (he had trench mouth) and was incarcerated in a venereal ward for four and one-half months. Some months later he was admitted to officers' candidate school at Camp Lejeune, North Carolina, and at Quantico received his commission as second lieutenant, United States Marine Corps. During his last week of training the atom bomb was dropped on Hiroshima, and Styron, like his buddies, was ecstatic at this reprieve from death. The moral implications of the bomb would come to him later. Ordered to duty at the Disciplinary Barracks on Hart's Island in the New York harbor, Styron guarded the naval prison for only a few months before the Japanese surrendered and the war was over. He was discharged from the military, went home to Newport News for a visit with his father and stepmother, and returned to Duke in March 1946.

The postwar atmosphere at Duke University, more free and

relaxed, created a favorable environment for the flowering of the writer's artistic talents. Styron's grades improved markedly, and under the tutelage of Professor William Blackburn, a member of Duke's English department, Styron resumed the creative writing that had been interrupted by his call to active duty. His first story had been "dubiously submitted" (as he signed it) to Blackburn in 1943, yet it was well received by the teacher, who commented encouragingly, "A sincere and beautiful story, ably told. You have got to the inwardness of your subject + that is poetry." Gradually Styron gained confidence in his abilities. During the summer of 1946 he attended the Breadloaf Writers' Conference and wrote an account of his trip to Trieste as assistant veterinarian on a cattle boat; this "Moment in Trieste" saw print two years later in *American Vanguard*, a publication of the New School for Social Research in New York. He published eight short pieces in Duke's literary magazine, *The Archive*, from 1944 through 1946 and absorbed from Blackburn the sonorous rhythms of seventeenth-century prose that would later characterize Styron's own work.

Blackburn became Styron's friend and mentor. In 1947, recognizing that Styron would soon graduate and seek employment, he encouraged his prized pupil to apply for a Rhodes scholarship on the strength of his creative writing. Styron was one of two finalists from North Carolina—it could not have hurt his chances that Blackburn was chairman of the selection committee—but did not make it through the southeastern regional competition in Atlanta, a victim of his pertinacity in failing physics. On the train home to Durham, Styron got drunk after his first experience with bourbon and missed his stop, awakening in a small town near the Virginia border; feeling joyful in spite of this dislocation, Styron imagined himself even farther north, in New York City, casting his lot with creative writing rather than with teaching.

Upon graduating from Duke in the spring of 1947, Styron moved to New York City and took a position as associate editor at Whittlesey House, the trade book department of McGraw-Hill. The title meant very little: Styron's job was to read the endless slushpile of manuscripts for a net gain of $34.50 a week. (In this pile was *Kon-Tiki*, which Styron rejected, a tale he tells on himself in *Sophie's Choice*.) Simultaneously he took a creative writing course at the New School, taught by Hiram Haydn, then an editor at Crown Publishers. After only six months at Mc-Graw-Hill, Styron was fired from his job. By some accounts the grounds for dismissal included such unprofessional, irreverent habits as sailing paper airplanes and plastic bubbles out the window and refusing to wear a hat. Perhaps Styron's general youth and inexperience simply did not sit well with the brand-new editor. At any rate, from that time on, with veteran's compensation and support from his father, as well as with encouragement from Haydn, Styron devoted all his efforts to becoming a writer.[3]

In New York, living with a former roommate from Duke, Styron began to write *Lie Down in Darkness*, first titled *Inheritance of Night* (which name it bears in *Sophie's Choice*). The book was based partly on his own private agonies and partly on the rootless country-club life of his small southern town. The first pages poured out easily, without the necessity for revision; they so impressed Haydn that he took out an option on the book for Crown. But Styron soon developed writer's block and returned to Durham in late 1947 to see if a change of setting might help. There, surrounded by familiar southern cadences and scenes, Styron began another novel, about life in the military, but left his first one untouched. Hiram Haydn urged a return to New York, and after almost a year in Durham, Styron made his way north once again—this time for good—and settled into a boarding house overlooking Prospect Park, in the Flatbush section of Brooklyn. He struggled to complete *Lie Down in Darkness* but found himself able to work steadily on the book after moving to Valley Cottage near Nyack, New York, the home of a writer friend named Sigrid de Lima, whom he had met in Haydn's class and to whom he eventually dedicated his novel. A later stay in an off-Broadway apartment shared with a Jewish friend brought Styron into contact with the Jewish urban milieu that characterizes the final section of the book. Early in 1951, before Styron had finished his work, he was recalled to active duty; happily, Haydn's intercession with the Marine Reserve Board resulted in a three-month deferment and the completion of the

novel: the climax of the novel, Peyton Loftis's interior monologue, was done in less than six weeks (but cost Styron fifteen
pounds). Since Haydn had by now become editor-in-chief at
Bobbs-Merrill, *Lie Down in Darkness* was published by that company. Haydn's letter to book sellers prior to publication heralded
it as "the most exciting literary event in the country since the
advent of Thomas Wolfe."

Meanwhile, Styron was stationed as a first lieutenant with
the Second Marine Division at Camp Lejeuene, North Carolina.
A reluctant soldier, he considered the Korean War to be, if not
without reason, then probably valueless. He spent much of the
summer enduring the heat and military orders—one long march
would be memorialized in Styron's next work—and was discharged late in the season because of a congenital cataract that
prevented his aiming a rifle properly. Shortly afterwards his first
novel was published to excellent reviews, and at the age of twen-
ty-six Styron found his book on the best-seller list along with
two other now-celebrated first novels: J. D. Salinger's *Catcher in
the Rye* and James Jones's *From Here to Eternity*.

Lie Down in Darkness was well received by the public, which
snapped up some 28,000 copies less than one month after publication. The *Saturday Review* included Styron among eight promising first-published authors in the United States. In April 1952,
Styron's literary colleagues recognized the author's promise by
awarding him the prestigious Prix de Rome Fellowship of the
American Academy of Arts and Letters; the jury was composed
of such well-known figures as Malcolm Cowley, John Hersey,
Van Wyck Brooks, Allen Tate, and W. H. Auden. The Prix de
Rome entitled Styron to three thousand dollars and a year's
room and board at the American Academy in Rome. Styron set
off for Europe in the spring of 1952, touring England and Denmark and sojourning in Paris before settling down in Italy in
October. Interestingly, another of Hiram Haydn's writing students—none other than Sigrid de Lima—won the Prix de Rome
the following year.

In spring 1952, Styron began a lifelong love affair with
France. After an initial bout with homesickness, he found in
Paris a congenial and nourishing environment for his art, and

formed friendships with an expatriate American literary community that have lasted until the present. One of Styron's new friends, Peter Matthiessen, whose Montparnasse apartment was a mecca for the newly arrived, conceived the idea of forming a literary magazine—and a group composed of Matthiessen, Styron, George Plimpton, and others set about seeing that idea to its fruition. The *Paris Review* was born of these efforts in spring 1953. The first issue began with a "Letter to an Editor" by William Styron, concerning the function of literature in this era and the aims of the new quarterly. The five thousand issues of the magazine sold out quickly. The fifth *Paris Review*, published a year later, contained an interview with Styron conducted by Matthiessen and Plimpton, and he was the first of the "young writers" to be so interviewed.

Not long after his arrival in Paris, Styron read to his new friends the whole of his latest work, written in six summer weeks—a twenty-one thousand word story first entitled "Like Prisoners Waking" and then "Long March." The reading lasted two hours and stunned at least one of the listeners, George Plimpton, who had no firsthand knowledge of *Lie Down in Darkness* or of Styron's reputation. The novella was first published in the February 1953 issue of *discovery* magazine, a new periodical anthology of original writings coedited by Vance Bourjaily. It was reissued four years later in book form by Random House (Haydn's new firm) in a Modern Library edition. The title then, as now, was *The Long March*. In 1957 the work was featured in the anthology *The Best Short Stories of World War II*, published by Viking Press.

Styron left Paris for Rome and the American Academy in early October 1952. In Rome he renewed his acquaintance with Rose Burgunder, a poet from a socially prominent Jewish family in Baltimore whom he had met earlier in the year in a seminar at Johns Hopkins University. Rose was a Wellesley College graduate with a master-of-arts degree in creative writing from Hopkins. The two were married in Rome on May 4, 1953. Styron has said that as a rebellious Protestant he sought his balancing opposite in a Jewish mate. In more than thirty years of marriage the Styrons have raised four children, three girls and a boy, the first

(Susanna) born in 1955 and the last (Claire Alexandra) in 1966. Rose Styron has continued to write poetry and is active in Amnesty International, the group that monitors human rights violations worldwide.

Following their marriage the Styrons spent a few months in Ravello, Italy, where Styron started a novella about his experiences as a prison guard on Hart's Island. But seven thousand words into the story, he left off working on it. Instead, he began to use his more recent experiences in Ravello as a source for a new work, a novel about an American movie crew in Italy much like the one he had observed there. (John Huston was making *Beat the Devil* in Ravello at the time.) The main character lives in the basement of a palazzo, just as the Styrons did. Styron continued work on this novel after his October 1954 move to the white-frame house in rural Roxbury, Connecticut, where the family still lives. Characteristically he stayed up late drinking Scotch and playing Mozart on the phonograph, reserving the afternoons for writing. Whether because of or in spite of this regimen, Styron completed *Set This House on Fire* five years later, and it was published on May 4, 1960, the Styron's seventh wedding anniversary.

The book was not fundamentally well received by the American critics (the *New Yorker* review was entitled "False Alarm"), and within a year it was remaindered by the publisher because of unprofitable sales. In France, however, it was widely acclaimed, having been translated by Maurice-Edgar Coindreau, an important critic who had been William Faulkner's first literary advocate in that country. The publication of *Set This House on Fire* in France in February 1962, as *La proie des flammes*, stimulated the French reading public to reconsider Styron's first novel as well. He has been designated a major writer in France—indeed, in all of Europe—ever since. In 1973–74, *Lie Down in Darkness* appeared on an official list of English readings required for all French doctoral candidates. Styron was the only living author on the list, in the exclusive company of Shakespeare, Hawthorne, and Poe. He has since been invited several times at the request of French universities or the government, and considers the French attitude toward artists to be enlightened and nourishing.[4]

By the 1960s, with two long novels and one short one to his credit, Styron had become well known in the United States. He began to appear on panels and to participate in symposia, such as the first inter-American symposium on the arts sponsored by *Show* magazine in 1962. He also covered William Faulkner's funeral for *Life* magazine and attended a White House dinner for Nobel Prize winners. In 1966 he lectured in Egypt with Robert Penn Warren, and was one of four writers selected that year as a member of the Department of Literature of the National Institute of Arts and Letters.

In the *Saturday Review* for February 1952, which had identified Styron as a promising author, the young man had listed no hobbies but many interests, including history and politics. There he had characterized himself as an "intrusive liberal," abhoring intolerance but unwilling to fight actively against it or to work for any political cause. In the sixties, however, Styron did put on the fighter's mantle, taking up journalistic writing to espouse a variety of causes. For example, he campaigned for Eugene McCarthy, advocated equal rights for blacks, spoke out for academic freedom, and lambasted political persecution of writers in Spain and the Soviet Union. A piece on Benjamin Reid, a condemned black man from Connecticut, appeared in the February 1962 issue of *Esquire* to argue against the death penalty. Four months later, Styron noted with some satisfaction that Reid's sentence had been commuted, and that his article in *Esquire* had stimulated the pleas for clemency. Styron continued to produce articles and book reviews throughout the decade, for such journals as *Harper's Magazine* and the newly formed *New York Review of Books*. He also edited a volume of short stories from the *Paris Review* and worked on a screenplay with George Plimpton about a murdered freedom fighter in Alabama. In April 1964 Styron was named Honorary Fellow of Silliman College at Yale University.

Meanwhile, Styron was fulfilling a long-standing dream, the creation of a novel about Nat Turner. Turner, the nineteenth-century black firebrand, was one of William Styron's earliest interests. Reading Virginia history as an elementary school pupil in the rigidly segregated South of the 1930s, Styron came across a notation about Turner's short-lived but bloody insurrection one hundred years earlier, in Southampton County not far from Styron's own home. As a high school student, Styron played football and basketball in neighboring Courtland, once called Jerusalem, the place where Nat Turner was hanged. There, the sycamore "hangin' tree" was pointed out to him. Over the years, as he matured, Styron became fascinated by the slave who alone in the annals of black-American slavery had carried out an organized revolt.

In New York in the late 1940s, Styron had contemplated writing a novel about Nat Turner, but Hiram Haydn convinced him that he was not yet ready to tackle the subject. So Styron wrote instead on a topic he knew more about: domestic relations among suburban Virginians. However, Nat Turner's role in American history had not been forgotten. The January 1952 issue of *Mademoiselle* announced Styron's intention to write a novel about Turner. Styron wrote from Paris at that time to tell his father that Turner's rebellion would be the subject of his next novel, and to ask for reading matter on Nat Turner in particular and in general on Virginia history of the period. With material supplied by a professor from the Hampton Institute, supplemented by conversations with novelist James Baldwin about black life in America, Styron set about his work. Twenty years after he had given up the attempt to capture Turner in words, feeling inexperienced for the task, he completed his novel before daybreak on January 22, 1967. The following spring and summer were spent in Italy and France, recuperating from the ardors of writing the book.

The novel was published by Random House on October 9, 1967. *Harper's* had heralded the event by devoting its September issue to a fifty thousand word excerpt (for which Styron was paid more than any writer in the history of the magazine to that time). The timing of publication was either fortunate or unfortunate, depending upon one's point of view. An occupation of Styron's for almost the whole of his life to that time, this meditation on slavery appeared in a turbulent decade of racial conflagration. Understandably, the work created an enormous stir. Many critics quickly dubbed the main character "Styron's Nat" or "Styron in blackface." Indeed, the novel was often referred to as "The Confessions of William Styron."

The culmination and distillation of this controversy was a book of essays entitled *William Styron's Nat Turner: Ten Black Writers Respond.*[5] The exceptions taken by black critics to the writer's work were many. Primary among them were the charges that Styron, a white man, had appropriated a black hero; that he had changed and distorted the facts to suit his purposes; and that these alterations reveal an insidious racism. Styron responded to these charges by insisting that Nat Turner was never a real black-culture hero. Furthermore, not much is known about him, and, in any case, the novelist is in no way bound by the historic facts, but may alter them as he sees fit to create his unique account. Styron's purpose was to give a picture of what slavery was like, as well as to rid himself of the last vestiges of his southern-white legacy of racism.

Reviews of *The Confessions of Nat Turner* from the established press were excellent, and the novel became a best-seller—Styron's first real commercial success. In 1968 the novel was officially recognized for its artistic achievement by the Pulitzer Prize Committee, which awarded it the prize for fiction. Another honor came in 1970: the Academy of Arts and Letters bestowed upon Styron the Howells Medal, given every five years for the most distinguished work of American fiction published in the preceding half decade.

In the 1970s Styron continued to produce essays that were, as he later characterized them, offshoots of his "occasional crochets or perennial preoccupations." He reviewed a prisoner's account of life in a Florida jail and, for a book about an accused teenage murderer, wrote an introduction that rails out against the inequities of America's judicial system. He also reviewed literature that came out of the Vietnam era, and reflected on the honor, courage, and atrocities of war. His play, *In the Clap Shack,* based on his own incarceration in the venereal ward of a naval hospital, was produced by the Yale Repertory Theatre on December 15, 1972, and published by Random House six months later. A screen play entitled "Dead!", coauthored with John Phillips, appeared in the December 1973 issue of *Esquire.*

In the early seventies Styron was hard at work on a war novel called *The Way of the Warrior*, a fictional treatment of his own experiences during the Korean War. The novel went slowly as he struggled with it, publishing portions in *Esquire* and *American Poetry Review*. Finally, in 1974, after many years of work, Styron abandoned the novel in favor of a more compelling idea. One night he awoke from a dream about a woman he had met years earlier, in the summer of 1949, when he had lived for a month in a boarding house in Brooklyn. Styron was then attempting to write *Lie Down in Darkness*, but suffered from a writer's block severe enough to prevent his writing a word. Here he became acquainted with another resident of the boarding house, a beautiful Polish survivor of Auschwitz. It was this woman whose image later pushed aside Styron's war novel: ironically, his creative energies were renewed by this remembrance of an earlier time of blocked literary urges. Styron worked on *Sophie's Choice: A Memory* for several years, doing research on the concentration camps and visiting Auschwitz as, years earlier, he had visited Southampton County in Virginia, for inspiration and a sense of the physical and psychological landscapes. He completed the book in late 1978. Excerpts appeared in *Esquire*, and the novel was published on Styron's fifty-fourth birthday—June 11, 1979—under the shortened title *Sophie's Choice*. It was dedicated to his father, his most loyal fan, who had died the year before.

Sophie's Choice was another commercial success, on the hardcover best-seller list for forty-seven weeks. Reviews of the book were mixed, but the balance tipped toward praise, and the novel won the first American Book Award for Fiction in 1980. In July 1981, movie producer Keith Barish announced the casting for a large-budget production of *Sophie's Choice*. The film premiered in December 1982, when the book was in its tenth printing. Directed by Alan Pakula, it starred Meryl Streep and Kevin Kline; the screenplay was written by Pakula, with a few suggestions from Styron, and Meryl Streep won the Academy Award for Best Actress for her portrayal of Sophie. This motion picture is the first made of a Styron work. (An effort had been made to film *Nat Turner* a decade earlier, but the controversy surrounding that novel stymied the filmmaking in its earliest stages.)

Following the publication of *Sophie's Choice*, Styron continued to publish essays and reviews. He assembled a volume of his short nonfiction under the title *This Quiet Dust and Other Writings*. The collection contains pieces on a variety of familiar Styron themes as well as autobiographical glosses on his fiction and bows to his literary ancestors and friends. He also returned to his uncompleted novel *The Way of the Warrior*. Originally, Styron set his action in Camp Lejeune, North Carolina, and Japan during the Korean War. By 1982 he was fifty thousand words into the revised work and preparing for a field trip to Nicaragua: the novel then focused on a marine colonel obsessed by a crime he had committed in Nicaragua years earlier, and was intended, according to the author, as a "parable of the United States' nosy involvement in places like Latin America." By 1984, Styron was describing the novel somewhat differently. In what Styron hoped would be the final stages of composition, *The Way of the Warrior* concerned the last military engagement in World War II and the last man to die in combat on Okinawa. The narrator—the same Stingo of *Sophie's Choice*—was to be saved from combat and probable death by the dropping of the atomic bomb, just as William Styron had been saved from a Japanese invasion years ago. Like *The Long March*, Styron's sixth novel would deal with soldiers caught in the war machine, prey to the military bureaucracy. It also would examine class in America. A portion of this novel, called "Love Day," appeared in *Esquire* for August 1985.

A bout with severe clinical depression, including hospitalization on the Yale-New Haven psychiatric ward, resulted in the complete restructuring of *The Way of the Warrior*. Progress on the novel had been agonizingly slow, full of false starts and blocked turns; Styron's frustration with it was not unrelated to his breakdown. In the winter of 1986, after his release from the hospital, Styron realized that his focus on the second world war was a wrong direction—he had to link that war with Vietnam. As he told novelist Philip Caputo in late April of that year, the revised version of *The Way of the Warrior* would show how "Vietnam was a logical offshoot of post-World War II America. It was inevitable, because our entire national identity was bound up in its relationship to worldwide communism." Styron approaches the subject through the relationship between a crippled Vietnam veteran and his father, a lieutenant in World War II and a zealous foe of communism. The complete alteration of the novel will add another couple of years, Styron estimates, to its composition.[6]

Buoyed by a passionate determination to make strong statements—a determination that requires considerable patience and energy—Styron, now past sixty, continues to devote years to the creation of his ambitious, substantial novels, recreating what he calls the "thickness of experience" in dense, highly textured prose. That he considers the writing of fiction to be a painful, even horrendous task is no doubt a function of his subject matter as well as his style: Styron's novels deal with thorny moral, philosophical, and psychological issues, and with the depths of human degradation. Yet his setting pencil to paper is itself a testimony to the resiliency of the human spirit and the necessity for people to communicate. Novelist Walker Percy (whom Styron greatly admires) recounts the story of Kafka's reading *The Trial* aloud to friends, who roared with laughter, to illustrate that the act of writing, even if the works are agonized and despairing, is a gesture of affirmation: "To picture a truly alienated man," Percy says, "picture a Kafka to whom it had never occurred to write a word."[7] Styron has written many words in his career and will write many more before he is through. The chapters that follow attempt to convey the shape and intent of Styron's major works to date.

2

A Dream Denied:
The Confessions of Nat Turner

All of a sudden I realized that all my work is predicated on revolt in one way or another. And of course there's something about Nat Turner that's the ultimate fulfillment of all this.

—*Newsweek*, October 16, 1967

William Styron's upbringing in the rigidly segregated South of the early twentieth century has repeatedly turned the author's thoughts to that "forbidden other," the black. The relations between the races figure to a greater or lesser degree in all his fictional works, for Styron has fixated almost obsessively on a people whose lack of acknowledged presence in the South paradoxically made them a prime preoccupation of many southern white writers. In an essay of the 1960s called "This Quiet Dust," about his interest in nineteenth-century slave Nat Turner, Styron remarks that the southern white often boasts of knowing the black, but in fact has only a superficial knowledge.[1] What Styron felt as a moral mandate to come to know the black person, rather than merely to observe him, impelled the writing of *The Confessions of Nat Turner*. By dedicating it to his black yard man, Styron intended to give recognition to all American blacks, previously isolated from white society by the laws and customs of segregation—a people who had little existence for the southern white of Styron's youth except as servants.

Styron had little biographical information to work with, since facts about the historic Nat Turner and his slave revolt are not readily available. A five thousand word pamphlet called "The Confessions of Nat Turner," by Thomas Gray, Turner's court-appointed lawyer, purports to transcribe Turner's words

17

after his imprisonment. Published shortly after the execution, it provides only a partial (if reliable) contemporary picture of the man. The few newspaper accounts of the period are sketchy and conjectural, in the absence of telegraph and railroad. The Southampton courthouse records contain mere listings of the personages involved. The single scholarly book on the subject, by William Drewry, a doctoral candidate at Johns Hopkins University, was produced almost seventy years after the event. Exerting what he considers his prerogative as a novelist, Styron applied his imagination to the meager facts about Turner and fleshed out a life for this shadowy historical figure.

In the early 1950s, a professor at the Hampton Institute had sent Styron a copy of Drewry's *The Southampton Insurrection*, published in 1900 and autographed by the author in 1905. Styron relied heavily on this account of Turner's rebellion when he began his novel a decade later. In reading this study carefully, he found clear evidence of a white Southerner's bias that belied the study's epigraph, a quotation from Quintilian translating as "History . . . written to narrate not to prove." Styron reads Drewry as maintaining the principle of white supremacy. Indeed, Styron finds more admiration for Nat Turner in Thomas Gray's pamphlet, in spite of Gray's obvious prejudice, than in Drewry's supposedly objective account (Some modern critics, ironically enough, have found more admiration for Turner in Gray's work than in the theoretically sympathetic treatment by Styron[2]). Styron himself had many points to prove in his novel, including the white race's complicity in the Turner rebellion and the lengths to which the human spirit in bondage will go in order to free itself.

To make his points, Styron saw fit to change or ignore some of the alleged facts about Turner's life that he came across in Drewry's study. His annotations to *The Southampton Insurrection* highlight Drewry's references to Nat's son, and to the theory that Turner's parents helped him learn to read; a note on the flyleaf suggests that Styron believed Turner had a wife. Styron creates a different but not unbelievable Nat Turner—wifeless, childless, dependent upon his owners for an education. More isolated from black society than the slave portrayed by Drewry, Styron's Nat is left almost totally rudderless when abandoned by his white benefactors. Without ignoring the details of slave life in the 1830s, Styron freely adapts the life of a particular historical personage in order to underscore the consequences of American racism in any era. One of Drewry's quotations from Gray elicits Styron's most impassioned marginal note: watching Turner receive his death sentence, lawyer Gray remarks, "clothed with rags and covered with chains, yet caring to raise his manacled hands to heaven, with a spirit soaring above the attributes of man. . . . [M]y blood curdled in my veins." And Styron responds, "In this sentence . . . is summed up—like I think no other sentence in American history—the horror, the actuality of our bloody past, and possible future."[3] Styron's self-described "meditation" on history is also a description of the racially explosive time in which he wrote the work and a warning to the generations to follow.

The Confessions of Nat Turner is a meditation in another sense as well, since the main character broods on the events of his life and the meaning to be extracted from them. Styron writes in the first person, as a condemned black man sitting in his jail cell on the day of his execution in November 1831, telling part of his story to his lawyer and recollecting the rest. For this quasi-auto-biographical mode of narration, a favorite technique of Styron's, he took a direct cue from Camus's *The Stranger*—also told in the first person by a condemned murderer in his jail cell on the day of his execution—which he read at his Martha's Vineyard home in 1962. Styron's Nat means his confessions not as an atoning for sins committed, since he does not acknowledge them as such until the very last, but rather as a recounting of the motivations for his rampage. The horrible mutilations and slaughter have already occurred as the novel begins. The previous August, Nat Turner and more than forty followers had murdered sixty whites, including women and children. The "what," therefore, is known; the "why" remains to be discovered. Speaking as Nat, Styron reconstructs through a series of flashbacks the incentives for these events.

There are actually three "confessions" in this novel: the historic document by Thomas Gray, phrases of which are directly incorporated into Styron's text; Styron's imagined account of

Turner's statements to his lawyer, which provides the frame of the novel; and the thoughts and remembrances of Nat, which he relates not to Thomas Gray but rather to the reader. In the last of these, Nat eventually reveals the reason why the kindest white masters are targeted for extinction. Styron thus implies that the few known "facts" of the case, as set down by Gray in 1831 from Nat Turner's testimony, are themselves only questionably authentic and certainly inadequate to account for the massacre. Only by a gradual peeling away of circumstances can the truth of the issue, what lies beneath and sometimes seems to contradict the facts, stand exposed.

It was liberating for Styron to get out of his limiting white self and to imagine himself as a black man, just as it is liberating for Nat Turner, confined in his jail cell, to range widely in his thoughts while circumscribed in space. Whether critics of *The Confessions of Nat Turner* have applauded or lambasted Styron's efforts, all agree that it was a bold stroke for Styron to tell the story as Nat himself. In the words of Yale professor C. Vann Woodward, who interviewed Styron in 1967, "We know that historians can tell what it was like to have slaves, but not very much about how it was to be a slave. That is, I think, what you have tried to do, without, of course, being either a slave or Negro yourself." Styron reinforced Woodward's point by noting how astounding it was that a particular real-life slave was available to him as a persona:

After all, when one considers the total anonymity of slavery one would find oneself hard put, I think, to become any slave: I happened to be able to turn myself into this almost unique slave, one of the few slaves in [American] history to have achieved an identity. . . . That is, the number of slaves whom we can remember can be counted on the fingers of one hand, and Nat Turner happens to be one of them.[4]

Although, by comparison with the deep South, Virginia slave life was not odious, it nevertheless reduced the blacks to ciphers or nonbeings. Nat Turner bears the surname of his owner, a common occurrence betokening the submergence of the black into the dominant white culture. The slave was simply part of the decor, as it were, of white life, uncredited with human thought or sensibilities, or with the possession of a private self. Thus, Nat's mother is forced into sex with the Irish overseer by a broken bottle held at her neck—her home and her body accessible to those in power. Nat's grandmother has enjoyed even less autonomy and control. An African who has gone insane from early captivity and childbearing, she is buried in the slave graveyard under a cedar headboard carved with the name "Tig." Nearby markers bear other white-given names suitable for house pets, names like "Peak" and "Lulu" and "Yellow Jake." When the cemetery grounds are needed for the cultivation of sweet potatoes, "Tig" and the others are denigrated further by being reduced to fertilizer for crops, their markers cleared away, their existences unceremoniously and completely obliterated. The last human refuge or private space, the grave, has been invaded.

In an underclass of anonymous creatures, the one tiny spark of freedom possessed by the nameless can quickly be gutted if it draws unfavorable attention. So Nat Turner early discovers that the best form of protection from the white person's whims and cruelties is to remain as undifferentiated as possible from his fellow slaves. He and the others talk "nigger talk" to the whites, subservient, flattering, and humble. But Nat Turner, by virtue of his caretakers' aspirations for him, is not like the other blacks—which accounts for Styron's interest in him and, more fundamentally, for his knowledge of him. Nat's mother, a house slave who looks down on the field workers, believes her son to have special talents and abilities. His master, Samuel Turner, teaches him how to read. The double existence Nat leads is well expressed by the doubleness of his language. Although his discourse with both blacks and whites is conducted in the aforementioned "nigger talk," his thoughts are expressed in the poetic and elevated terms of an educated man. He thinks, in fact, the way Styron characteristically writes, in complex sentences with a polysyllabic vocabulary. If, as some believe, Styron's expression of Nat's thoughts is unrealistic for a slave who has learned only how to read, it nevertheless is an apt symbolic reflection of Nat Turner's unacknowledged—and unacknowledgeable—rich inner life, and of his desire for elevated status in society.

Turner approaches a fatal crossroad in his life when he acts

on his yearning for education. By stealing a book from his master, and asserting (not quite truthfully) that he can decipher its
contents, Nat at age ten becomes the object of Sam Turner's
experiment to prove that a slave is educable. Whether he was
made a victim or a beneficiary of his master's good intentions is a
question that Nat often asks himself in his adult years, especially
as he awaits execution. Even favorable attention from the white
race has a potentially negative effect, raising unfulfillable expectations simultaneously as it cuts a person off from the support of
his own race and class. Nat's ability to read elicits only resentment from his fellow slaves and provokes mistreatment from the
virtually illiterate white man, Thomas Moore, who eventually
purchases him. Released from the anonymity of slave life
through education, and promised his freedom as a result, Nat
Turner finds his hopes frustrated because society as a whole
cannot keep the promises made by a few individuals. The gap
between promise and fulfillment is a chasm into which the so-
cial-climbing Turner falls. Ultimately, the tensions between Nat's
love for his people and hatred of the whites, and his scorn for his
people and admiration of the whites, create the fatal flaws in his
personality—the divided self—that drive him not only to rebellion but also to ruin.

Total frustration of hopes and expectations accounts for one
strange fact that lawyer Gray is determined to have his client
explain: why the kindest masters were slain while the cruelest
were spared. This is a question that the historical "Confessions" asks by implication but cannot answer. Jeremiah Cobb is,
second to Sam Turner, the most outspokenly sympathetic white
to the plight of the slaves, yet his recognition of the incipient
personhood of every slave, and his rantings against the institution of slavery, arouse in Nat a great deal of hostility as well as
fear. Judge Cobb is powerless to act in any meaningful way on
his humanistic inclinations. He raises hopes in any slave to
whom he reveals himself, and any slave worldly wise enough to
understand that those hopes must inevitably be dashed will
want to kill him for his sentiments. Remembrances of Cobb's
exhortations provoke Nat Turner's comments on "the central
madness of nigger existence," and the central paradox that the

kindest slave owners have been murdered. Utter cruelty toward and subjugation of the black ensures his loyalty to the oppressor, but a "hint of philanthropy" inspires him to whip out his knife: "tickle him with the idea of hope, and he will want to slice your throat." This notion, revealed early in the novel, is repeated over the course of Nat's story, in different circumstances, and it is one key to the mystery of human personality that Styron painstakingly unlocks.

To Styron, then, the idea of hope proffered by the white and then snatched away before fulfillment is a prime motivating force behind Turner's insurrection. The daily indignities of slave life as depicted by Styron and the historians whose studies he consulted would seem to provide ample motive for rebellion, but in fact few rebellions were fomented in the history of black slavery in America and none except Turner's reached full fruition. In his novel, Styron describes two small-scale revolts in order to counterpoint Turner's feat and to suggest its rarity. Both of these actions are individual rather than group efforts and they are largely ineffectual. In an effort to maintain his pride, Nat Turner's father runs away after being slapped by his master; the reader does not learn his fate, but his absence from Nat's life is assuredly a cause for Nat's eventual fixation upon Samuel Turner as well as for his own desire for rebellion. The escape attempt of Nat's best friend, Hark, occupies a long and poignant section of the novel. Knowing only that he needs to find the Susquehannah River in order to flee northward, Hark stumbles along for six weeks believing himself to be ever closer to his goal. However, Hark's meager knowledge of geography leads him not to the "Squash-honna" but ironically to the James, mother-river of slavery, mere miles away from where Hark began his exodus. There he is captured and turned in—by a black man. Hark's story encapsulates both the strength and the futility of a slave's desire for freedom, and with its meaningless circularity—reminiscent of Sysiphus pushing a rock eternally up a hill, never to be rid of his burden—it aptly conveys the absurdity of human existence.

The strong, innate desire for freedom and autonomy manifested by Nat's father and friend is contained as well in Nat himself, whose streak of rebelliousness against a stultifying caste system is a quality admired (and shared) by Styron. To this motivation Styron adds the motif of betrayal to account partially for Nat Turner's rampage. The reader learns early on that Turner has felt dislike for many, but actual hatred for only one man. Although the man is never named, the circumstances of Nat's life lead to the reader's discovery that he is Samuel Turner, Nat's chief benefactor and savior, who is also the central betrayer of hope in Nat's life as Styron imagines it, and therefore the central destroyer. Sam Turner's betrayal is even described centrally, about halfway through the book—a culmination of all that chronologically precedes it and an explanation for all that is to follow.

After seventeen years of slavery that have fostered his complete, childish dependence on white society, Nat Turner is promised freedom in Richmond after he turns twenty-five. Nat feeds on this promise even as he witnesses plantations breaking up because of the increasingly depleted tobacco economy, and slave trains moving south for cotton picking in Georgia or Mississippi. He feels himself set apart from his peers, in spite of one slave's warning that "Yo' ass black jus' like mine, honey chile." Even when Sam Turner in desperation begins to sell off his own slaves, and has Nat deliver them to slave traders, Nat clings to the hope of his own eventual freedom. Eventually Sam Turner dissolves his mill and moves his family to Alabama, leaving Nat under the "protection" of a seemingly kind minister until he is old enough for life in Richmond. That things work out rather differently from what the well-intentioned Samuel Turner had imagined is at first an incomprehensible mystery to the teenage Nat and later the source of an all-consuming rage. The dream of freedom, at first only deferred, is at last denied, and Nat can never forgive his master for holding it out before him. Although he never sees Sam Turner again, and although he believes that he has put Sam Turner completely out of his mind, Nat moves toward his vision of bloody insurrection out of desire for revenge against this once-beloved father figure. The eventual murder of the kindly master Joseph Travis is explainable largely on these terms.[5]

Another motive for Nat's insurrection is sexual repression.

Indeed, Styron weaves throughout Nat's narrative the motif of sublimated sexual urges as a primary component of the revolutionary impulse. To the extent that Nat's sexual problems are a result of his being a black in white society, these problems are racial in essence. Significantly, it is a gesture of pity by a white woman for an old, shuffling freed slave that arouses in Nat an almost uncontrollable lust, so inextricably bound with Nat's insurrection are his hatred of the kindly white and his view of sex as an act of domination and humiliation. Then, too, Margaret Whitehead parades in front of Nat in her underdrawers, without consideration for his feelings as a human male. She is looking for a certain poem to check whether the correct citation is *endurance* or *forebearance*; yet it is Nat who must have forebearance in this situation, so that he might endure. Nat is also privy to the white owners' sexual secrets—like Emmeline Turner's tryst with her cousin Lewis—without having an outlet for his own urges. No compatible black woman is available to him nor is slave society conducive to stable marriage.

On the other hand, Nat's sexual problems may have as much to do with his nationality as with his race. As Styron has remarked, "Nat is a man who could not have existed anywhere outside of America, even if he were white. His problems are truly American; even his sexual hangups and difficulties are American in outline [i]n the sense that there is a residual Puritanism, a conflicting Calvinistic sort of frustration . . . because he is the product of an era in American history."[6] Nat firmly believes that the Lord commands his stifling of fleshy desires in order to attend singlemindedly to the desires of the spirit for God. Thus, he fasts and also avoids women, occasionally resorting to masturbation. With no one but his friend Willis (or his own body) does Nat ever enjoy actual tender sex, and these moments are followed or even accompanied by guilt.

Nat's longings for Margaret Whitehead, as both a man and a slave, are important for understanding why he murders her and only her during the hours of rampage. Margaret is not deliberately provocative, but she affects Nat as she would any man and he must struggle to overcome lust, fear, and loathing. As with Samuel Turner, her closeness and her liking for Nat constitute

hope proffered but unfulfillable; her tantalizing nearness is in
essence a mirage. Because Nat cannot have her, he simultaneously hates and loves her. When he later goes on his rampage he
runs after the escaping Margaret Whitehead because he wants
her in two senses: she is the object of both his desire and his
vengeance.

Turner's complex motivations for rebellion include not only
social and sexual factors but a large religious component as well.
From earliest childhood, Nat is designated as a visionary because he is able to recount events that occurred years before his
birth. Believed to have been set aside by God to become a proph-
et, Nat takes to fasting and prayer and avoids the company of
ordinary society. Eventually he becomes a self-ordained preacher, in whose personality religious fanaticism predominates. In
his eyes, the uprising that he conceives in his adult years is part
of God's plan, outlined in the prophetic exhortations of the Bible. Designating himself as nothing short of an Old Testament
avenger, Nat feels kinship with the furious prophets who received their messages directly from God.

In fierce contrast to Nat's adherence to Old Testament prophetic writings, and to explain its genesis and force, Styron
depicts—sometimes scathingly, sometimes subtly—the vagaries
of orthodox Christianity as practiced in Virginia at the time.
Several denominations come in for the author's attack. Every
Mission Sunday, Nat and the other "darkies" climb into the
balcony of the Methodist church to hear minister Richard Whitehead preach a sermon composed especially for slaves by the
Methodist bishop of the state. This actual sermon, portions of
which are incorporated into the novel, commands the blacks to
serve their masters well on earth if they wish to be free men in
heaven, and it portrays God as the ultimate taskmaster. Richard
Whitehead shows a similar lack of charitableness toward socially
unacceptable members of his own race by refusing to baptize
Ethelred T. Brantley, who eventually finds his salvation through
immersion by the slave preacher, Nat Turner.

The Episcopalians are portrayed as no more "Christian"
than the Methodists. In his youth, as Samuel Turner's slave, Nat
is taught to read by drilling in the Episcopalian catechism. His

lessons turn on such sentiments as man's being only a little lower than the angels. But the traveling Episcopal clergymen quote a different kind of scripture for their own purpose, justifying slavery as the best and necessary form of existence for a morally deficient people. The only Episcopalian to argue with them against slavery is Sam Turner, who admits that he is, after all, not very religious.

The Baptists fare no better under Styron's pen. The Reverend Alexander Eppes, to whom Sam Turner consigns Nat when the mill is dissolved, turns out to be a morally deformed human being, making sexual innuendos to his new slave on their first meeting. He compensates for his frustrated sexual desires for Nat by working him mercilessly, especially on Sundays. About the Baptist worship services Nat is circumspect, only hinting at their perversity: whipped into a frenzy by the rantings of their preacher, the congregants strip down to their underwear and ride each other's backs up and down the aisles.

In between the bacchanalian worship of Reverend Eppes and the decorous approach to religion of Richard Whitehead are all gradations of Christian practice and thought. The novel is suffused with religion, as southern society, both black and white, was at the time. Margaret Whitehead, Richard's teenage sister, attends a seminary dedicated to the so-called Christian education of females, an education in the fine arts and a finer spirituality. She finds in Nat Turner a companion for discussion of the Bible; he is the servant who carries her to church both literally and figuratively. Meanwhile, university professors of Christian theology, like the Episcopal clergymen, demonstrate what they term the predestined inability of the black to make moral choices. They find justification in the Christian religion for the continual subjugation of the black race. Styron shows that the only Christian sect with a clean record on slavery is the Quakers. Of course, Thomas Gray ridicules them for their view of the malignancy of this institution. Such a misguided attitude, he explains to Nat, is representative of true northern ignorance.

As he awaits execution, Nat faces a crisis of belief. His lawyer, himself a nonbeliever, reminds Nat continually of the devastation wreaked by his Christian zeal: not only the casualties of the rebellion itself but also the extermination of more than one hundred innocent blacks by a rampaging white mob in retaliation for the uprising.[7] Nat cannot reconcile these turns of events with his sense of a God-ordained mission. After speaking to him regularly, God is noticeably silent for Nat in his prison cell. He feels alone and cut off from the only guidance and sustenance he believed he could count on. Before, Samuel Turner was to Nat a father-God, at the very least a great biblical hero like Joshua or Gideon, and at the most, God himself. But with Turner's abandonment of Nat at the door of the perverted and cruel Reverend Eppes, Nat has grown disillusioned with the promises of humankind. He has transferred all his faith to the heavens and acted out what he has seen as God's commandments as written in Holy Scripture. Yet his acts have served only to estrange and isolate him from the Divine Spirit. Prayer itself is now impossible. Something is very wrong. The prison cell that incarcerates Nat is a metaphor for the narrowed hope and spiritual darkness of a man removed from God.

In Nat's jail cell, Thomas Gray speaks to him of the necessity for affixing blame for the murders. Unlike a runaway wagon that kills a child, Nat is considered animate chattel possessing moral choice and spiritual volition. Of course, Gray's reason for taking this view is to absolve the masters of complicity in these killings; nonetheless, Styron would agree, the aforementioned theologians to the contrary, that all human beings must accept some responsibility for their deeds, no matter how dominated they are by others. The ultimate degradation would be to live like an insect, driven by instinct toward one course of action or another. Although Nat in his despair thinks of the blacks as flies, without the will to free themselves from their condition, in fact Nat and the others live as humans with the ability to make choices even in their circumscribed lives. Nat has made his way through a seemingly determined sequence of events leading to insurrection and bloodshed, but his freedom of will has flickered even in the midst of darkness and deprivation. The responsibility for his estrangement from God must ultimately rest with him.

Indeed, the victimized Nat Turner, in Styron's opinion, has become a victimizer himself. To a large extent he detests his fellow slaves and looks down upon them, his attitude having been formed by his privileged (relatively speaking) position in white society and fostered by his aggrandized self-assessment as a *person* as well as a black person. Nat does not even realize that he is a slave until the age of twelve, when Samuel Turner's brother uses the word in reference to him. The word chills his bones as a child and inspires him as an adult to exert control over the other slaves and therefore to assert what he sees as his special and unique qualities. Pursuing his own visions leads him to misuse his authority. He takes pains to keep the other blacks in his dominion. Even his religious activities, like the baptizing of Willis, express his own powers as much as the Lord's. And when Miss Nell Turner presents him with a Bible at Christmas time, the sight of the field slaves straggling up to the Turner place for their own gifts fills him with intense loathing for these creatures that is at least equal to his resolve to redeem them from death. Nat's "higher consciousness" leads to the cultivation of hatred not only for his own people but especially for the whites of Southampton County. Although he bases his determination toward their widespread slaughter on a mandate from the Lord, Nat is surely driven by private, self-centered concerns (the evils of slavery notwithstanding). In this sense, Styron focuses on Nat Turner less as an actual historical personage, a rebel slave in nineteenth-century Virginia, than as a human being whose activities widen rather than narrow the gulf between himself and God.[8]

The importance of Nat's quest for God cannot be overestimated. Because of the racially explosive times in which the novel was published, *The Confessions of Nat Turner* has been analyzed largely in terms of the black-white issue. But from the first, Styron has maintained that he meant the work not only as a reflection of a certain historical period but also as a religious allegory. Styron views the book as "a story of man's quest for faith and certitude in a pandemonious world, symbolized by bondage, oppression and so on." Perhaps if he had published it two decades earlier, when he'd first thought of doing so, critics might well have emphasized the protagonist's religious torment and cited the influence of a writer like T. S. Eliot. But as it happened, the civil rights movement and contemporary problems of the 1960s tended to obscure an important element of the work, what Styron himself terms the "symbolic representation of the conflict between the vengeance and bloodshed of the Old Testament and the redemption, the sense of peace and renewal, of the New Testament."[9]

The New Testament possibilities within Nat Turner are suggested by parallels with the life of Jesus Christ. Nat is in his early thirties at the time of his rebellion. He is a carpenter, apprenticed to a Mr. Godt. Because of Nat's lack of education, he imagines his employer's name to be spelled *goat*, thereby conjuring up in the reader's mind the connection between Christ and the goat, or scapegoat, of more ancient religions. Nat actually has a vision of his mission to take up Christ's burden of bringing salvation to humankind. In reality, Nat is made a scapegoat for the sins of the larger white society; his deed arouses a tremendous outrage and serves to cleanse the whites of their responsibilities for these crimes. His march to prison through throngs of hostile onlookers is reminiscent of Christ's stations of the cross, especially because of the real-life place names with their appropriately symbolic connotations: As Nat trudges toward the town of Jerusalem, from Cross Keys, the whites spit in his face, kick his back with their boots, and pierce his shoulders with hat pins.

By the end of the novel, through his recollection of past events, Nat is able to approach God again before his execution. He achieves redemption through remembrance. Having acted from the idea that murder is necessary for freedom, and that God has ordained this violence and bloodshed, Nat continues to be troubled by the one murder he has managed to commit personally—that of Margaret Whitehead. Somehow this murder is connected to the absence of God in Nat's life, and somehow, almost in spite of himself, he must make atonement for this murder in order to reach at-one-ment with God.

After reconstructing all the reasons for his actions, rehearsing the many indignities and even atrocities visited upon himself and his loved ones throughout his life, Nat cannot, finally, justify his murder of Margaret Whitehead. He remembers that on their last outing together, a few weeks earlier, he and Margaret had come across a turtle crushed by a passing wagon. Margaret had suffered with the turtle's suffering, and Nat had killed it with a hickory branch to end its agony even though he did not believe that such dumb creatures can suffer: "They that doesn't holler doesn't hurt," he had told her. Nat's murder of Margaret is symbolically linked with the incident of the turtle. He has been unable to kill anyone else—mysteriously, the ax has missed its mark with the Travises and others, and his primary henchman has had to finish the tasks—but he can indeed kill Margaret. His motives, as already stated, are mixed. He needs to commit this murder to maintain his control over his men; equally important, his revenge on Margaret Whitehead is in essence his revenge on Samuel Turner as well, for both have tantalized him with dreams incapable of realization; finally, his sword thrust beneath Margaret's breast is an act of symbolic rape. However, added to these motives is the mercifulness to put Margaret out of her suffering after his first blow maims but does not kill her. Nat acts out of a kind of Christian charity, responding to her whispered plea for death; for those who don't holler may indeed hurt. Did Nat lose or find his humanity at the Whitehead farm? Styron muses (in "This Quiet Dust") about this gruesome scene.

In a sense, Nat plays out the last act of the masque that Margaret had once enthusiastically described, in which the pagan Philemon, converted to Christianity by the lovely Celia, plights his troth with her by holding up his sword in front of her like a cross, while she swoons into an eternity of love. Nat begins to repent for his murder of Margaret almost as soon as he commits it. He almost hears Margaret's schoolgirl voice prattling earnestly about an eternity of love, and he recognizes his violent act with her as a fulfillment as well as a parody of Philemon's troth with his beloved. As he aimlessly circles Margaret's body shortly afterward, Nat lets a young girl escape almost in retribution for this life he has taken.

The book ends, therefore, with Nat's dreamlike revelation of the New Testament ideals of charity and love. These ideals were voiced daily by Margaret, whose presence was so important in Nat's life—not solely as a Delilah or temptress, as he saw her, but also as a Beatrice or spiritual guide. When Margaret had appeared before Nat in her pantalettes, provoking both his lust and his rage, she had been seeking a library volume of Wordsworth to check a quotation from the Lucy poems: the stanza she reads aloud to Nat is about "a perfect woman, nobly planned, / To warn, to comfort, and command; / And yet a spirit still, and bright, / With something of angelic light." Styron no doubt means these sentiments to apply by extension to Margaret herself, whom Nat belatedly comes to see as a saving force. Called from his prison cell to approach the gallows, Nat hears God speaking through the voice of Margaret Whitehead, entreating him heavenward to a reconciliation of opposites in love. At the last, Nat is able to communicate with God. The message he receives is Styron's vision of unity among classes, races, and genders.

Resurrected through Nat's memory, Margaret Whitehead becomes a hostage for his soul's ransom. So, too, by resurrecting Nat Turner through his novelist's imagination—by meditating on history—Styron creates a hostage for the ransom of his own soul. With some playfulness as well as guilt, Styron suggests that his own ancestors may well have been among those invited to Samuel Turner's parties: guest lists for these gala affairs include planters from Virginia and North Carolina with names like Clark, Styron's grandmother's name. By viewing the white race from a black person's point of view, in *The Confessions of Nat Turner*, Styron not only enacts a narrative tour de force but also attempts to expiate the sins of his ancestors and free himself from the racial bigotries of contemporary society.

3

~~~~~~

In Search of Order:
Lie Down in Darkness

It seems to me that human beings are a hair's breadth away from catastrophe at all times—both personally and on a larger historic level.

—*New York Times Book Review*, December 12, 1982

Lie Down in Darkness begins with a paragraph composed of a single long sentence conveying the sweep and distance of a train trip from Richmond to Port Warwick, Virginia. Styron cleverly puts the reader in that swinging, speeding passenger car through the use of the word *you*—a strategy, appropriated from Robert Penn Warren's novel *All the King's Men*, that is designed to draw the reader into Port Warwick (read "Newport News") from whatever town he inhabits, and hence to compel him into the lives of the Port Warwick residents whose stories lie ahead. The reader, in effect, becomes a resident of the town for the duration of the novel, and its characters become neighbors or acquaintances whose activities are the stuff of both scandal and tragedy.

The introductory pages of the novel provide transition, then, from the real world inhabited by the reader into the imaginary world of Styron's art. After these scene-setting descriptions of Tidewater landscapes and accents, Styron deposits the reader at his destination on a hot summer day. The novel proper, switching to the third person, begins on a weekday morning in August 1945—the date, the reader soon infers, is symbolically appropriate—when a group of people arrives at the Port Warwick station to meet the train from New York carrying the body of a beautiful young suicide. Styron withholds for several pages the name of the

33

victim, her physical description, and the fact that she has killed herself. He begins with the tantalizing arrival of a corpse, slowly presents the details to round out the picture, and thereby draws his own variation on the familiar southern theme of a family's disintegration. In anatomizing the suicide of this young woman, Styron anatomizes upper-middle-class life in suburban Virginia and comments as well on modern American life in general. Throughout the novel, the psychological atmosphere is as oppressive as the unbearable physical heat in this first scene.

One by one Styron introduces the important figures gathered at the station: Milton Loftis, the distraught father of the dead woman; Dolly Bonner, his fatuous, devoted mistress; and Ella Swan, longtime black retainer of the Loftis family. Although she is not present at the scene, because she refuses to come, Helen Loftis, Milton's estranged wife, is very much present in the concerns of all the others. And, of course, the dead Peyton Loftis is central.

Peyton Loftis's funeral provides the frame of the novel. The events of the present take place over a few hours in a single summer day. As he awaits the train, Milton's thoughts flash back to earlier occurrences in his life, and from these fragments of remembrances Styron weaves the fabric of his book. The hearse transporting the body continually breaks down, and at each hitch in the process, each cessation of forward progression, time stops and then reverses. Like the movement of the hearse, then, the past unfolds in fits and starts, in chronological disorder. Styron has jumbled the time sequence partly as an artistic challenge, one that creates a certain tension in the work,[1] and partly as a means of realistically representing human thought processes. His distinctly modernist technique is an effective counterpoint to his characters' search for order.

Styron's complex narrative strategy is to present a series of interior monologues that bump up against each other, as it were, bruising instead of connecting. The reader has to do all the work at connection, penetrating first one mind then another (five minds in all), finding in the jumble of memories and concerns the interlocking pieces that create a patchwork quilt of intermeshing lives. For the individual characters memories do not comfort or sustain: recollection fails to re-collect these broken lives and piece them together. But the reader creates a kind of order, reconstructing the past through the thoughts of Milton, Dolly, Helen, Carey Carr (Helen's minister), and, finally, Peyton herself, with some assistance from direct authorial narration. Both intimate and distancing, Styron's narrative structure elicits sympathy from the reader while maintaining his objective judgment on events.

Milton Loftis is the character for whom the reader tends to feel the most pity and frustration, since his aspirations are more exhaustively rehearsed than the others'. Milton's grief is almost as palpably suffocating as the dust that falls on the mourners at the station, and almost as searing as the hot summer sun. Milton feels cheated by life, tricked and defeated by the destruction of his hopes for the future embodied in his beloved child. The continual breaking down of the hearse constitutes a nightmare version of his own life, an inability to reach a destination. This failure to move smoothly forward frames a myriad of failures in Milton's life, failures ranging from the domestic to the political.

Self-pity is the primary emotion in all of Milton Loftis's ruminations. Things have never turned out well for him because the events of his life have not, he thinks, been under his control. He feels victimized by outside forces. A central figure in Milton's musings is his deceased father, who had spoken in Latinate phrases—and speaks still, in memory—of the necessity for gentlemanliness, honor, and self-control. But Milton's tendencies toward reckless behavior manifest themselves early. The freedom of college propels Milton not into responsibility but into profligacy, His father eventually secures for him a safe commission in the army's legal branch, and so he escapes combat in World War I. Marriage to a West Pointer's daughter achieves for him an officer's rank, and his wife's inheritance allows the establishment of a law practice and a comfortable, country-club life in Port Warwick. His memories of a sustaining father-son relationship are suffused with the odor of the grand cedars that lined the approach to the elegant Virginia home of his youth. Memories of conjugal bliss are accompanied by the fragrance of the gardenias filling romantic summer evenings. But Milton's nostalgic yearnings for an unrecoverable past are overshadowed by perverse resentment toward his father and his wife for their many gifts to him. The father has left him through death, though their estrangement preceded that event; long separated psychologically from his wife, Milton leaves her two years before the opening scene of the novel.

From the reader's first glimpses of Helen Loftis—through Milton's remembrances of their courtship, and through the undertaker's vision of her living room—the impetus for Milton's attraction to her, as well as her unsuitability for him, is apparent. Helen is a sober, prudent, conventional woman, disapproving of Milton's wild ways. She seeks and achieves order, at any price. Where Milton is blubbery with emotion, Helen is cool to the point of coldness; where he retreats from pain into liquor, she takes to her bed in sleep or hypochondriacal illness. From her point of view, she has been a suffering martyr for years because of her husband and her children. Thus she refuses Milton's plea—made in an agony of grief over Peyton's death—to take him back into her home and her heart. Milton remembers and wishes to recapture the Eden of their younger married lives, when Peyton was a child and life offered such promise. But Helen's remembrances are different, and full of bitterness and gall.

Styron constructs the novel around several long, dramatic scenes that center on Peyton at different stages in her life. The incident with the bees, recounted in the parents' memories of Peyton's childhood, provides one example of many failures at communication and connection. Milton refers wistfully to the time when Peyton ran screaming from the bees at her relatives' home in Pennsylvania. Peyton was young and beautiful and innocent; she believed that her father could protect her from all forms of danger. Milton contrasts this idyllic time with the agony of the present. Helen, however, remembers the incident differently. As Peyton escapes the bees, Helen feels maternal concern and warmth for her child as she rises to protect and comfort her. Milton, however, rises from his chair more quickly and, intercepting Peyton, carries her off to safety—a knight and his damsel, shutting off the rest of the world. The incident frustrates and hurts Helen, who senses her superfluousness; it is she who is stung. In reaction, she stiffens toward Peyton, and the child, sensing the coldness, the resentment, and the hostility, forges her bond with her father even more decisively. In consolation, Helen reinforces her own bond with her crippled and retarded elder daughter, Maudie.

Peyton is so central to this story, and to Milton Loftis, that the reader does not find out about Maudie until entering the mind of Helen. Peyton has always been a threat to Helen. The child's youth and beauty are painful reminders of Helen's own advancing years and lack of centrality in her husband's life. Excluded from a relationship with this daughter, Helen retreats into a relationship with the older one, whose physical and mental deficiencies make her less attractive to Milton. Maudie is safe—she poses no threat to her mother. Moreover, Maudie needs constant care and thereby gives Helen a feeling of usefulness. With her limited capacities, her care is physically taxing but emotionally undemanding. She remains a child forever, and thus Helen need not deal with the adolescent turbulences and physical flowering of a normal female. Indeed, Helen romanticizes Maudie and wistfully looks to her innocent, over-the-fence fascination with a workman who performs magic tricks as the apotheosis of romantic love. With her sexual coldness and her fear of being supplanted, Helen idealizes Maudie as the perfect child.

In contrast to the placid Maudie, Peyton is a complex individual whose behavior calls for a real parent rather than a mere caretaker. At the age of nine, Peyton and Melvin Bonner (whose mother will later become Milton's mistress and whom he is even now courting) play a game and tie up Maudie, almost suffocating her. Styron only suggests that Peyton releases her own hostilities in this "game." What he makes perfectly apparent is Helen's reaction of outrage at the deed. She slaps Peyton, calls her a devil, and then retreats to her customary place of refuge, which is the bedroom. Later, hand in hand with her father, Peyton goes to her mother to ask forgiveness for her sin. The alarm clock ticking in the darkness and Helen's hands like "seabird wings" may well be the sources of the two recurrent images in Peyton's adult fantasies: the clock, as a symbol of order, and the birds, betokening sin and guilt. After the moment of expiation with her mother, Peyton goes out on the town with Milton almost as if out on a date. As Helen lies alone in her bedroom, Milton snuggles with his nine-year-old daughter on a joy ride in their car. These situations and the relationship they epitomize are unnatural and even perverse.

On the evening of Peyton's tying up Maud, Milton makes his first real overtures toward Dolly Bonner, whose overt sensuality attracts and excites him. Helen, of course, is not blind to these overtures, a fact that figures into her overreaction to Peyton's misdeeds. Perversely jealous of her own daughter, Helen considers the nine-year-old to be sexually provocative, not an unrealistic assessment since Milton is clearly and exclusively interested in this child and reinforces certain of her behaviors. Later, the reader discovers that Milton has attempted intimacies with his small daughter. At least, Peyton hints at these horrible occurrences on the day she takes her life, and events witnessed by the reader through the course of the novel leave little doubt as to the truth of these memories. On the day Peyton is married, for example, Milton pulls his daughter to him and forces on her lips a wet, blubbery kiss. Peyton pushes him away in disgust, but Helen once again attributes Milton's behavior to Peyton's provocativeness. After Milton's affair with Dolly reaches fruition, Helen has dreams of seeing Dolly dead, but eventually realizes with a shock that the legs of the dead dream-rival are Peyton's rather than Dolly's.

Milton Loftis is attracted to Dolly Bonner because her interest in him contrasts so sharply with that of his icy wife, who considers him a selfish husband and an inadequate breadwinner. With some sense of relief as well as guilt, Milton turns to Dolly for a feeling of kinship and self-worth. Dolly, the wife of a mere insurance salesman, admires Milton's country-club social standing and is attracted to his facility with words. Indeed, she is seduced by Milton's poetic though empty speech (which Helen sees through) because it represents to her a certain high culture and romanticism. Beguiled by Milton's spouting of poetry, she eventually succumbs to his advances and lies down with him in the darkness of the country-club golf museum during

Peyton's sweet-sixteen birthday party. As usual, Milton is drunk, for whiskey softens the tawdry edges of this episode as it softens all the harsh edges of Milton's life, adding a romantic glow to the decidedly unromantic and removing the years that have aged and disillusioned him.

If, through drink and sex, Milton momentarily recaptures a glimpse of a lost Eden, for Peyton the episode marks the loss of her own innocence. Eavesdropping on her father and Dolly at the door of the museum, she senses the destruction of her childhood; Styron symbolizes this expulsion from Eden by having her lie down nearby an abandoned playground. (A similar scene occurs in *Sophie's Choice*, when the no-longer-innocent Stingo returns to the empty amusement park.) Peyton's birthday party takes place in August 1939, the day before World War II begins. Port Warwick reads the war news in the papers but, in a festive mood, cheers the launching of a pleasure ship from the Port Warwick dock. That night the Loftises hold their party in honor of Peyton, and a domestic tragedy plays itself out while warfare looms "offstage." Two years later, Milton and Dolly playfully refer to the date of Milton's divorce from Helen as D-Day. And the climax of the family's downfall—Peyton's suicide—takes place the day after the Atom Bomb is dropped. (Styron originally set the year as 1946, but later changed it to 1945—specifically, August 1945—in order to reinforce this connection.) Styron thereby sets the family's ultimate loss of innocence in a larger context, linking it, without irony, to a grandly global fall from grace. *Dramatic* irony—in which the reader sees flaws the characters overlook—is created by the community's self-indulgent inability to gaze beyond its hedonistic pursuits.

The twin themes of disintegration of the nuclear family and destruction of countries through warfare and nuclear holocaust are rounded out by the portrayal of decay of an intermediate level of social organization: the community. The hearse passes through the marshlands of Port Warwick, redolent of decay and pollution, on its way to the cemetery. More than a mere setting for the action, Port Warwick itself is an important presence in the novel, as a negative force: it is to be defined by what it can no longer provide—sustenance. Life for the upper-middle-class

whites centers around the country club, but this is a center
which, to use Yeats's words, cannot hold. Social and religious
institutions cannot muster the vitality of the country club, yet
the club vitality is only feverish and brittle. This community, if it
may be called that, is indifferent toward how people live their
lives, and this indifference frees its members from adherence to
restrictive moral codes.[2]

On the day of Peyton's funeral, Milton Loftis whiningly pro-
tests that outside forces have buffeted him, forcing his life—as he
sees it—into certain patterns. In actuality, Milton has had many
choices to make. His affair with Dolly, for instance, takes six
years to reach its official start, since Milton does not force it to a
head, mostly out of a residual feeling of propriety. But once he
knows that Helen is aware of his feelings for Dolly, Milton becomes lost in a dark wood of moral indecision and cannot any
longer discern right from wrong. Thus he gives up the attempt at
trying and decides that there is no way to stop what he has
begun. Instead of setting Helen straight when she accuses him
of an affair with Dolly—instead of apologizing for the stolen kiss
and comforting his wife—Milton lets his guilt overwhelm them
both and push him into a very unwilling liaison with the other
woman. Falling back on the principle of determinism and thereby absolving himself of responsibility, Milton commits himself to
Dolly Bonner.

Helen Loftis, too, has had many chances to effect a rapprochement with her husband, but her pettiness drives them
even further apart. On the day before Peyton leaves for Sweet
Briar, Helen participates in and enjoys the excitement of her
child's going off to college. She intends to accompany the family
to Sweet Briar the following day. But as she watches Peyton and
Milton interacting, from the inner sanctum of Maudie's room,
she feels a stab of jealousy and resentment, even hatred, and
these emotions lead her to take senseless affront over a meaningless exchange with Peyton about a hat. In turn, she resolves to
stay home the next day. Shortly afterward, Peyton lets Maudie
fall—perhaps by accident, perhaps not (the reader cannot be
sure, any more than Peyton herself can be sure[3])—and Helen
uses that event as an excuse to stay home. She takes solace in her

gardening, creating order by plucking, weeding, and throwing away the broken pomegranates. Her Garden of Eden is bereft of an Adam, however, and Helen is powerless to face down the snake of her selfishness and hatred. Yet even in his portrayal of this most unsympathetic woman, Styron grants Helen grains of humanity that prevent the novel from tipping wholly toward Milton. On the day of Peyton's funeral, when Helen realizes that this is the first day she cannot call herself a mother, the reader feels for her sympathy mixed with despair.

Throughout the course of their married lives, Milton and Helen attempt to affix blame for their domestic tragedies. What caused Maudie's retardation and paralysis? Who is at fault for Helen's coldness or Milton's affair with Dolly? Who can be blamed for Milton's need to drink? And, ultimately, where does responsibility lie for Peyton's suicide? Is one of the protagonists at fault, or is this all a trick of God? Do humans have free will or are their actions determined by chance or even design? Are children helpless in the face of their parents' deficiencies or can they extricate themselves from the unsatisfactory patterns laid down in their childhood? Helen, Milton, Peyton—each tries to discover where the trouble started, to find the way out of the labyrinthine web that constitutes their tangled lives as a family. And the bit players in this tragedy, Carey Carr and Harry Miller, also try to determine what went wrong and why. Because of Styron's narrative technique—incident recounted within incident, flashback within flashback—it is as difficult for the reader to get to that first cause, and thus affix blame, as it is for the characters themselves. There seems to be no single cause, but rather many faults distributed among many different personalities, all contributing to this web of hostile interdependencies.

The disintegration of family relationships is charted and highlighted by a series of festive occasions, opportunities for family solidarity that raise expectations for a new start. Inevitably the old, familiar patterns reappear, destroying the illusion of solidarity and exacerbating the customary tensions that the family has attempted to conceal. Each event seems an especially cruel dashing of hopes, plunging the family ever deeper into the hell of hatred and despair. Styron organizes his novel around ceremonial, almost cinematographic scenes.[4] As already stated, the funeral of Peyton provides the framework. Additionally, Peyton's growing up is captured in a series of potentially happy milestones that turn into crises: the country-club dance and Peyton's going off to college are two such events. Still another is the Christmas holiday during Peyton's college years. Rather than providing an occasion for a joyful family reunion, this Christmas celebration illuminates and aggravates the conflicts among family members. Milton is jealous of his daughter's boyfriend, a student at the University of Virginia, whom she has brought to meet the family. He also resents Helen's brother, Edward, for his army colonelship (Milton is only an air-raid warden). Worst of all, Dolly calls Milton at home on Christmas Eve and Helen storms upstairs to bed in disgust. To cope with this upsurging of emotions, Milton begins to drink. Peyton, in turn, is greeted bitterly by Helen and flees the house for a party. Christmas Day therefore dawns drearily and the stage is set for disaster. Edward is called away by the army—this is December 1941, only three weeks after Pearl Harbor—and Milton is jealous of Edward's status and usefulness. Helen repudiates Peyton's Christmas greeting and accuses her of wanton drunkenness. She also acts the martyr in the preparation of dinner and for no accountable reason provides paper birthday hats for everyone, which they don after the childlike Maudie puts on hers. Peyton feels keenly the incongruity between the state of innocence betokened by the hats and the fall into experience known by all but Maudie: she rushes sobbing from the house and, in effect, from the family.

All that Peyton really wants is a home and family to support her. She continually and obsessively makes a quest toward this elusive Eden only to be repeatedly forced to flee. Milton makes the same futile gestures toward his daughter. In Charlottesville, where Maudie has gone with Helen for therapy, another such fiasco of missed connections plays itself out. Although Helen begs Milton to stay with her at the hospital, she does not permit him to confer with the doctor about Maudie's condition. Feeling excluded as usual, Milton succumbs to the urging of an old fraternity brother to drop by a University of Virginia fraternity house for a drink. He is motivated more by a desire for Peyton, whose boyfriend is a Kappa Alpha like Milton, than by the need for a drink. Once again, against the backdrop of a ceremonial, the stage is set for disaster: Milton's personal homecoming with Peyton, Helen, and Maudie becomes a farce of miscommunication and frustrated desires.

In a nightmare, the object of one's frenzied quest is always just one step out of reach. Likewise, Milton is maddeningly unable to locate Peyton at the fraternity-house party or the football game that follows. Milton chases after Peyton, who he learns has just gotten "pinned," from one place to another, but though he catches tantalizing glimpses of her, she always eludes him—symbolically, she's lost to Milton because she has committed herself to another love object. Suddenly he feels old and superannuated. Even Dolly Bonner's discarded husband, whom he meets by chance, has found happiness with another woman. Milton finally arrives back at the fraternity house after falling drunk into a culvert; the knight errant, bleeding and stinking, meets up with his princess at last. At the hospital, it is Peyton who bears the full brunt of Helen's anger. As Maudie lies near death, Helen reminds Peyton of the time she let her sister fall and accuses her not only of indifference to Maudie but also of wanton complicity in her father's absence from Helen's side. This is the familiar refrain in Helen's dealings with Peyton and, as before, at the Christmas celebration, the accusations drive Peyton directly to drink and to sex. What Peyton seeks is release from her mother; but, ironically, she becomes as incapable of real love as her mother is.

Needing love desperately—so desperately that she is unable to give it—Peyton cannot achieve a satisfactory relationship with her boyfriend, Dick Cartwright. She is aware of her failings, attributing them partly to a "Freudian attachment" to her father and partly to her parents' entire generation, which lost its children by unloosing the moorings with their stabilizing traditions. The relationship with Cartwright ends and other affairs follow, all tortured by Peyton's unfulfillable needs and by her all-consuming feeling of guilt. Hope for her emotional salvation arrives in the unlikely form of a New York Jew named Harry Miller, whom Peyton meets after leaving Virginia without graduating from Sweet Briar. Her wedding to Harry is to take place at the Loftis home, thereby marking not only their own union but also her parents' miraculous reconciliation, which had taken place not long after Maudie's death. At this grandest of ceremonials, which Carey Carr refers to as "the symbolic affirmation of a moral order in the world," Styron portrays the final disintegration of the Loftis family.

Milton begins Peyton's wedding day with hope. Helen has shown her soft, maternal nature in making gestures of reconciliation toward Peyton. Milton has cut down considerably on his drinking and has given up Dolly Bonner. Best of all, Peyton is home again, as beautiful and youthful as ever. The rich promise offered by life itself seems to unfold before Milton. The steady movement toward ruin and decay that his body has made, paralleling the events of his life, will be stemmed and then reversed by Peyton's marriage and the babies that will inevitably follow. For Milton, this day is one for burying all sadness, all memories of past failures and disappointments.

But the skeletons in this family's closet won't stay hidden, no matter how tightly the family bars the door. Peyton refuses to go along with Milton's pretense—or is it merely a wild belief or illusion?—that everything is fine in her family. Helen has not finally reached out in love toward her daughter but rather has created this spectacle of a wedding as a sign to the community of her forgiving and maternal nature. Deep down, amid her suffering martyrdom and her puritanism, amid her own buried resentments and fears, lies an intense loathing of her own flesh and blood. This loathing breaks forth when she observes Peyton pushing herself away from her father's smothering embrace. Helen's submerged feelings about Peyton's marrying a Jew, about Peyton's too-tight wedding dress, about Peyton's relationship with her father, about Peyton's being young and beautiful and embarking hopefully on a new life—all these feelings surface and lead to open warfare between the women. The final domestic battle has been fought, and Peyton flees again, this time forever, from her home. Milton flees as well, back to the patient arms of Dolly Bonner.

Throughout most of the novel, Peyton's life is filtered to the reader through the remembrances of her parents. But in a long section near the end Peyton comes alive, as Styron presents her thoughts directly, ironically on the day that she meets her death. The centrifugal pull of the novel draws the reader to her at last: having circled around her for so long, the reader now enters her mind and, through first-person narration, seemingly becomes Peyton, understanding fully for the first time the terrible force of her problems, the terrible weight of her past. This section is especially difficult to comprehend, for its disordered stream of consciousness, complete with occasional italicized portions, represents a disoriented individual. Careful attention is required for the reader to unpeel the layers of guilts and fears that culminate in Peyton's suicide. Her longing for a real mother is evidenced in the idealization of a great-grandmother she has never known, who used to hold Milton Loftis on her knee and call him "Bunny." Peyton dredges up memories of her own cold mother, who tells Peyton upon her first menstruation to read all about it on the Kotex box (so strong is Helen's puritanism, so deep her reticence in matters of sex). Having sought freedom from memory in New York and the sheltering arms of her husband, Peyton not only fails to escape the burdens of her past but even capitulates to her insecurities and jealousies, and so drives her husband away. With her, locked in her mind, the reader makes a last desperate search for order, buying a clock, symbol of harmony and perfection, a present to Harry to persuade him to take her back.

Peyton's monologue takes place as she journeys from her apartment to find Harry, making her quest for order and peace, forgiveness and love. To a policeman who stops her she explains that she is on her way to see Bunny. The momentary confusion indicates that her underlying search is for her father. Indeed, Styron precedes the novel with a quotation from James Joyce's *Finnegans Wake*: "Carry me along, taddy, like you done through the toy fair." These words might well be a plea from Peyton to her father, who has shielded her from harm throughout the toy-fair existence of her childhood. By the time she grows into adulthood, Peyton is unable to take care of herself. Were it not for Milton's overprotecting Peyton into softness, Helen's inability to

nurture her might well have made her tough. But since Milton
has taught Peyton to count on his making things right for her, she is
unable to develop those inner resources with which to sustain herself when her father-savior proves all too humanly ineffectual.

Peyton's final, tormented search for her father is the story in
microcosm of humankind's search for a Father God to guide
one's course through life. In her lovemaking with a neighbor on
the morning of her death, Peyton is very conscious of his St.
Christopher medal with the inscription, "*Travel Safely*. Jesus Savior Pilot Me." She later prays to Harry, "Give me my God back,
for somewhere I've lost my way." Throughout her life, the Lord
is hidden from her. Milton himself pleads to God, after running
from his responsibilities to Helen and the dying Maudie, to forgive his foolish son; but he is not sure that God is there to listen.
Even Carey Carr, the Episcopal minister, finds it difficult to
speak of the Lord any way but "wistfully," for the universe
seems to him intolerably empty and grim. The coda to the novel,
recording "Daddy" Faith's revival meeting, is at best only a tentative affirmation of God's presence on earth and may in fact
indicate the author's belief that religion can sustain the faith of a
child but not of an adult.

Lie Down in Darkness concerns modern humanity's childish
reliance on inadequate doctrines of authority. The novel explores
and rejects several traditional sources of value and guidance,
usually associated with fathers. Styron reserves the code of the
military as an object of close scrutiny for his second novel, *The
Long March*, but he touches on it in several places here, most
poignantly in Helen Loftis's remembrances of her cavalry-officer
father, Blood and Jesus Peyton, who insisted that he traveled in
the Army of the Lord. To his impressionable daughter, Blood
and Jesus was in fact God on earth, a severe god teaching strict
adherence to good soldierly conduct. Helen has learned from
her father to stick unyieldingly to a conception of herself as a
good wife and mother—hasn't she followed all the rules?—and
she sacrifices both Milton and Peyton to her notions of what is
proper. She is stiff and unyielding, refusing to compromise. Finally, she believes that she and she alone knows the meaning of
sin, and that therein lies her superiority to others.

Milton's own father represents yet another potential source

of value and guidance, the tradition of the Virginia gentleman. Milton recalls that when he went off to the University in Charlottesville, his father had advised him that "if the crazy sideroads start to beguile you, son, take at least a backward glance at Monticello." But Styron comments throughout the novel on the inadequacy of Mr. Jefferson as a Gentleman God, always implying that the religion of gentlemanliness is pap for babies. In the episode about Maudie's death, he presents old Mr. Dabney— who has made a pilgrimage to the hospital in Charlottesville in order to die near his idol—as a comic figure, hairless like a baby and treated like one by the nurse. In the very next scene, at the fraternity party where Milton hopes to find Peyton, a college girl complains about the gross attentions paid to her by "Virginia gentlemen, so-called," and her complaint is an ironic commentary on Milton's sophomoric and obscene pursuit of Peyton as well as on his perverted code of honor. Milton refuses his University of Virginia ring to his aptly named plaything Dolly—with whom he conducts a gentlemanly love affair—and gives it instead to the real object of his illicit affections, his daughter. The fact that he has deserted his wife and dying elder daughter in order to declare his love for Peyton indicates that he adheres to certain rules of conduct at the expense of more important, and more demanding, ones. As cynical New Yorker Albert Berger notes of southerners in general, Milton puts "manners before morals." He always represses the unsavory aspects of his life and plays a charade of propriety and grace. Appropriately, the souvenir ash trays being sold on the ferry from Port Warwick bear the legend, "Come to Virginia, Cradle of the Nation." Although Virginia is the birthplace of United States democracy, it also fosters the gentlemanly ideal that guides only the immature persons who cannot come to terms with their responsibilities.

The familiar and seemingly safe world ends on the global scale just before Peyton takes her own life. In her confused state, Peyton explains that the bomb has saved the world *from* democracy. The world of Peyton's past—the Virginia stretching out beyond even her father's memories, of stately houses, stately cedars, and stately ideals—has ceased to exist. Similarly, the premodern, preatomic universe has been shattered by a bomb on Nagasaki, killing one-hundred-thousand civilians. With no ideals or beliefs to sustain her, Peyton jumps from a loft in Harlem. Her death marks the end of the Loftis line, and the end of the Loftis hopes for eternal beauty and youth. Peyton's clock had jokingly been referred to by Berger as a time bomb, and the remark is symbolically apt: Peyton cannot reverse the passage of time and revert to a state of innocence. Her rudderless life was never Edenic, and she, like her father, is not strong enough to prevent a cataclysm. Similarly, Styron implies that the world has failed to live up to its promises, and is now immersed in chaos and despair, cut off from God and engaged in godless warfare.

For the Loftis family, the lacking ingredient is forgiveness. Helen has been ruthlessly unforgiving in her dealings with both Milton and Peyton, and Peyton in turn is ruthlessly unforgiving to Harry. His small indiscretions are major catastrophes to Peyton, for her enormous needs and dependencies make her vulnerable to slights and infractions of any degree. She runs from imperfections in her marriage, seeking not only vengeance upon Harry when she indulges in affairs with other men, but also new potential Edens. At the end of the novel, Milton's own hope for forgiveness from Helen is dashed when she refuses to come back to him. Capitulating to the seeming nullity of their existences, both Milton and Helen end up in this novel as they began, with nothing to sustain them.

In contrast to the white suburban Virginians, the black retainers achieve fulfillment of their life's quest for meaning and wholeness. Ella Swan, her daughter La Ruth, and La Ruth's son Stonewall have appeared throughout the novel in the background of the story as they are in the background of their employers' lives—cooking, sewing, and cleaning, taking stock of "their" white families but not generally taken much stock of in return. On the day of Peyton's funeral, the blacks of Port Warwick and environs are preparing for a communal baptism, led by Daddy Faith. In an early draft of the novel, Daddy Faith appears early on, but in this final version Styron wisely reserves him for the very last, his presence acting as a long-sought manifestation, almost revelation, of the godhead. Ella Swan is able to turn aside from her profound grief at Peyton's death by putting her faith in God; she approaches her baptism by Daddy Faith with hope and with joy, and her immersion brings her intense spiritual peace. The baptism, a more subtle frame to the novel than Peyton's funeral, is contrasted with Peyton's spiritual thirst and with her unallayable fear of drowning. For the blacks, the hardships of this life are mitigated by the promise of a better one, and the believers shake off their choking burdens of sin and guilt through religious ritual. For the upper-middle-class whites, religion is more of an intellectual, even social, exercise.

The train leaves Port Warwick for Richmond in the closing paragraphs of the novel, in effect bearing the reader out of the world that he has inhabited and come to know. (No doubt he leaves with some sense of relief. As Styron wrote in his own hand at the end of one early typescript, "These people give me the creeps.") A bleak vision of life remains. The bleakness lies not in the fact that death and decay are inevitable—the message of the epigraph from Sir Thomas Browne's "Urn Burial," echoes of which sound throughout the novel—but rather in that humans consistently make messes of the short time they have. Only a suggestion of the possibilities for redemption redeems this vision.

Styron implies an important role for art in the salvation of humankind. Milton Loftis is a poetaster rather than a poet. Though he loves poetry, he lacks the discipline of the true artist to create order out of chaos. In contrast, Harry Miller, Peyton's husband, is able to turn from his troubled life to the satisfaction of his easel. As a "disillusioned innocent" (his self-characterization), Harry uses the agonies of his life, and modern life in general, to create art that speaks eloquently to the struggle of humans to exist in the implied twilight of civilization. The old man in his portrait, proud and unafraid, stands amid rubble and gazes toward what Peyton describes as the "dying sun." The novel is Styron's portrait of that old man: the tenuous but real possibility for defiance of Helen and Milton's Nothing! Nothing! Nothing! Nothing! is repeated in the communication between human beings—between writer and reader—that is this book. Art testifies to belief; the creation of art is a holy act. *Lie Down in Darkness* is itself an intensely ordered depiction of chaos and a testament to the value of life and love.

4

~~~~~~

A View into the Abyss:
Set This House on Fire

I suppose the central pathos of the victim has always been a
central consideration in what I've written—the victimization of
people by life or by other human beings, sometimes even to the
extent that it has to do, at its most extreme, with slavery.

—The *Saturday Review*, September 1980

The flames of damnation threaten to consume the characters in
Set This House on Fire, and they lick at the feet of the readers who
step into this novel. So emotionally charged are the events, so
extreme the action, so fiery the language with which Styron
conveys it all, that casual skimming is not possible. We must
commit ourselves to pain and agony if we open this book and in
effect take the drive with the narrator into Sambuco, Italy, scene
of the central events. The novel begins innocuously, with a lyri-
cal guidebook description of the town. But it is soon discovered
that a few years earlier the peaceful Eden had been shattered by
shocking acts of violence, including rape and murder. In effect
Styron presents a murder mystery: the corpses have been discovered, and now it is to be determined "who done it" and why.
His use of a first-person narrator—an ordinary white, Anglo-
Saxon Protestant from Virginia—serves multiple purposes: it
draws us immediately into the story; it allows us to identify with
someone like ourselves; it distances us sufficiently from the cataclysmic events so that objective judgments on them may be
made; yet it also helps us to see the potential for violence and sin
in everyday lives.

Peter Leverett, the narrator, is a participant in the events of
the novel and functions as a central consciousness, but he is not

51

its central character. That role is played by Cass Kinsolving, an amateur painter who spends the greater part of each day drinking and playing the fool to Mason Flagg, a wealthy expatriate American. Peter and Cass meet each other in Sambuco, where Peter has gone to visit Flagg, his prep-school friend. The lives of these three men intertwine for a brief period and then abruptly separate after Flagg's death. About two years later, in America, Leverett and Kinsolving meet again to try to piece together the reasons for what occurred that summer night in Italy. Reference is made by Cass Kinsolving at the end of the novel to a man's getting truly started with his life when he moves toward *il mezzo del cammin*, or the middle of the way. This echo from Dante's *Inferno* reinforces the notion of journeying toward redemption by first descending into the pit. In this case, Peter Leverett plays Virgil to Kinsolving's Dante, guiding him toward knowledge of what went on during those hellish days when Cass was too drunk to know. Similarly, Kinsolving's confessions to Leverett allow this square and sober gentleman, a lawyer by profession, to glimpse dark recesses and disorders of his own self that he had never before fully acknowledged.

The structure of the novel is complicated. After an introduction much like the prologue to *Lie Down in Darkness*, in which the reader is escorted into a new environment—by train to Newport News in the first novel, by car to Sambuco in this one—the narrator, Peter Leverett, tantalizes his audience with hints of violent events, including rape and murder. The actual frame of the novel is a fifteen-day visit that Leverett has made to Kinsolving some years before in Charleston, South Carolina; they recapitulate the past then and for the first time come to terms with it. As is Styron's practice, the novel unfolds through flashback within flashback, with the two main characters revealing the bits and pieces of their lives that drove them together to participate in a summer night of madness. The past is reconstructed twice in the novel, in two sections, each with a different emphasis. Part 1 is about Mason Flagg: through Peter's recollections the reader learns of Mason's wealthy Virginian background; his rather perverse relationship with his mother, "Wendy-dear"; his sexual escapades, beginning in prep school; and his bohemian life in New York. These are facts about Mason that Cass never knew, and they help him to understand, if not to forgive, his adversary. Part 2 of the novel is Cass's account to Peter of his own background, and of his relationship with Mason. This account helps Peter to understand what he witnessed in Sambuco, to tie certain events together, and to draw them to a fitting conclusion.

The main events of this very long book occur in a single twenty-four hour period sometime in the 1950s, and they may be quickly summarized. Peter Leverett, who has been working in Italy, accepts the invitation of his old school friend Mason Flagg to visit him in Sambuco. On the way from Rome, Leverett collides with an Italian on a motor scooter, and though the accident was not his fault, he suffers through a police interrogation and imprecations by the cyclist's family. He arrives in Sambuco exhausted and troubled and immediately stumbles onto Poppy Kinsolving, her numerous children, and, finally, her slightly besotted husband, Cass. After a short sleep Leverett encounters a series of puzzling events. At a party at Mason's, full of phony Hollywood types who are filming a movie at the palazzo, Mason appears distraught and bloody after chasing a young woman down the corridors; he then proceeds to humiliate Cass as entertainment for his guests, and Cass is too drunk to demur or perhaps even to care. After intervening to stop the disgusting spectacle, Leverett is persuaded by Cass to join him in bringing stolen medicine to a dying Italian peasant many miles away. The hike further exhausts Leverett, and he falls into a deep sleep upon returning. When he awakens he learns that the girl he saw in the corridors of the palazzo has been raped and murdered. Mason, the assumed criminal, has committed suicide.

These are the facts, or the supposed facts. Into this gothic tale, replete with a lovely, ravished maiden and a dark villain, Styron weaves questions about the human condition that lift the story out of the realm of tawdry melodrama. One of the issues raised is the nature of evil. Specifically, both Cass and Peter are anxious to determine whether Mason Flagg was evil or sick or simply reprehensible. The question is not simply an idle one, for whiling away the hours during Cass and Peter's fishing trip in Charleston, when the fish aren't biting. Quite to the contrary,

Cass Kinsolving has an enormous personal stake in the answer, since, as he gradually reveals, Mason did not commit suicide after all but was thrown off a cliff by Cass himself. Even Peter— safe, sane, ordinary Peter—is anxious to affix a label to Mason, for he, too, has participated in Mason's activities to the extent of observing or hearing about certain vile practices but not attempting to stop them. If Mason was not starkly evil then Cass is a murderer. If Mason *was* evil, then Peter cannot excuse himself for failing to react more negatively. Both Cass and Peter struggle to understand Mason in order to understand themselves.

In fact, Styron hedges his bet here: on a symbolic level, Mason is a veritable devil who must be destroyed for the good of society; on a literal level, Mason is only a pathetic individual who has been misguided by America's false valuation of power and money. The novel proceeds, then, to tell several different stories at once. It is an allegory of a dark night of the soul or a pilgrim's progress, in which Cass Kinsolving comes to understand, and then to throw off, the evil part of his nature. It is also an account of the "ugly American" of modern vintage, patriotic to the point of ethnocentrism, flaunting his money and buying himself into the good graces of others, "doing his own thing" and exerting his will, heedless of the feelings of others. Then, too, it is a psychological case study of an attractive but sick young man who never grew up, held in thrall to his doting mother and never accountable for his actions. Finally, in terms of the outsider Peter Leverett, the novel records the shedding of innocent illusions and the movement toward a mature acceptance of sin, suffering, and death.

As a prelude to reliving the tragic events in Sambuco, Peter visits his hometown of Port Warwick, Virginia, where the "California influence" has resulted in such travesties as street names changed from Bankhead Magruder Avenue (with its reference to a Civil War soldier) to Buena Vista Terrace, and venerable magnolias, oaks, and elms replaced by Serv-ur-Selfs and Bauhaus-inspired churches. An overall deterioration in quality and rise in mediocrity stimulate Peter's father to diatribes against the decline of modern life in general. He predicts that the emphasis on the new, the shallow, and the thrilling will lead only to moral, spiritual, and political anarchy. What this country needs, he intones, is a tragedy on the order of the fall of Jericho, "so that when the people have been through hellfire and the crucible, and have suffered agony enough and grief, they'll be men again, human beings." Listening to his father, and revisiting the sites of his childhood, Peter Leverett realizes that in order to find out who he is, what he wants out of life, and how to get it, he must come to terms with what has happened in Sambuco. His visit to Cass to get (and give) the meaning of those events that occurred on foreign soil is the key to his understanding of modern life in the United States as well as his own place in that life.

The background information that Leverett supplies about his lfie in Rome before meeting Cass in Sambuco reveals a shallow and indulged individual. His lawyer's job for a government relief agency has him attending only to the complaints of fellow bureaucrats. His own complaints center around the poor quality of the commissary milk shakes, though his salary does enable him to purchase the other necessities of his life, primarily the snappy red sports convertible with which he later strikes the unfortunate Luciano di Lieto. His sojourn at the Sambuco palazzo of his boyhood friend Mason Flagg confronts him with his own tinsel existence writ large, as if he were looking in a fun-house mirror that distorts and enlarges but ultimately reflects the truth, however grotesque.

Leverett's entrance into this world is one of literal disillusionment. He strides into the scenic piazza and interrupts a man and a woman at their café table, only to discover that he has interrupted a staged event. Hollywood filmmakers have converted the town into one large set, as a consequence of Mason Flagg's long-time connections with the movie world. The movie being filmed is a modern-dress farce about Beatrice Cenci. This new American adaptation and prostitution of an old Italian tragedy is the equivalent in the world of "art" to Port Warwick's Glendora Manor housing development in the world of "architecture"—the California influence amounts to a selling of our American birthright and the selling out of our founding father's ideals.

The life of Mason Flagg epitomizes the worst traits of modern America as Styron sees them. Hyperbolically materialistic,

Flagg comes into Leverett's world at the age of sixteen, bearing cashmeres, golf clubs, Tootsie Rolls, and contraceptives. He boasts to his new prep-school friends of early sexual experiences, smokes English cigarettes, and charms everyone for a time, until his excessive lying turns away all the boys save one, Peter Leverett. Flagg's father is mostly absent, and his mother is a lush who attaches herself quite inappropriately to her teenage son. The boy is expelled from one school after another, and grows up to indulge in material goods as he has been indulged. A draft dodger, he makes deals to get PX privileges in Naples, carting to his palazzo great stores of meat and liquor and milk for lavishing on his guests and buying friends. He flaunts his enormous red Cadillac convertible in a land of extreme poverty, all the while denigrating the Italians for not speaking "the preeminent language of the world," English.

Peter Leverett is attracted to Flagg's way of life. His fascination with wealth and display is what keeps the friendship going in spite of the unsavory aspects of Flagg's character, and it is what pulls Leverett to Sambuco for the visit. The life that Mason Flagg lives there is as hollow as the production crew lounging about on his hospitality, as sham as the complexion and the name and the artistic talent of the hanger-on Dawn O'Donnell, as vacuous as the moral equation of wealth and virtue promulgated by another guest, the well-known Protestant clergyman Dr. Irvin Franklin Bell. Although Leverett recognizes the superficiality, and although he is repelled by it, he lets himself be "kept" by Mason Flagg in a sense. To Leverett, Flagg is more imaginative, intelligent, and entertaining than himself, but also more overtly corrupt, so that while enjoying Flagg's largesse, Leverett can still feel smugly superior. When he meets up with Flagg in New York, ten years after their prep-school days and four years before the Sambuco debacle, Leverett listens entranced to Flagg's tales of debauchery with a fourteen-year-old Yugoslavian girl, so overcome by the romantic word picture painted by the teller that he is only vaguely disturbed by the sleazy aspects of the story. The "square" in Leverett is a perfect complement to Mason's supposed avant-guardism in matters of life and art, which are hopelessly confused in Flagg's mind. To him, sex is an art form, endlessly staged because it needs a voyeur to be validated. He is more enamored of his collection of erotica than he is of any real woman; indeed, free and unbridled sex is for him only a cause, the one area left in life that allows men to express their individuality. Flagg's whole life is an elaborate artifice, an illusion. The "love of his life" is not, in fact, his wife, nor do his bits of trivia and arcana qualify as learning. He tells lies that pass for truth, he says, only to see if they will stand up as theater (but that, too, is a lie). His vaunted exploits in Yugoslavia never actually occurred, but were instead appropriated from a Rebecca West novel. Worst of all, Flagg beats his wife in secret. Yet in spite of Leverett's awareness of this chicanery and moral degradation, he accepts material gifts from Mason, "his old daddy," as a sort of bribe for friendship.

Only in Sambuco, watching Flagg command Cass Kinsolving to make a spectacle of himself under the guise of entertainment, do the scales of illusion finally fall from Leverett's eyes. Yet the kinship between Leverett and Flagg remains, a kinship deeper than liking, so that when Flagg is found dead at the bottom of a cliff, a supposed suicide, Leverett identifies him as his "best friend." In a sense, Flagg is Leverett's other self, the Mr. Hyde to Leverett's Dr. Jekyll. Flagg has lived out some of Leverett's deepest impulses and wildest fantasies, those that Leverett deprecates intellectually but feels drawn toward emotionally. Similarly Cass Kinsolving is bonded to Mason Flagg in an unholy matrimony, their marriage ceremony sanctified by Scotch in rites of blasphemous limericks, and celebrated in an environment similar to that of the ancient Roman circuses, in which slaves were pitted against each other in a fight to the death for the entertainment of the public ("We'll have us a circus," Flagg says to Cass). It is to free himself from this alliance with sickness and despair that Kinsolving throws Flagg off the cliff. What he discovers from Leverett's account of Flagg's past is that the man he has killed is a complex human being, deeply flawed but human nevertheless. Kinsolving has sinned deeply—against Flagg, Poppy, his children, and himself. The extreme nature of his acts require an extreme act of repentance in order for redemption to be attained. How Kinsolving fell into the pit of despair and degradation, and how he inched his way out of it, every toehold precarious, form the content of part 2 of the novel.

What one learns from Cass Kinsolving is that he, not Mason Flagg, has been his own worst enemy: "Kinsolving pitted against Kinsolving, what a dreary battle!" He has knowingly married a Catholic, and then, as she produces a succession of babies, he holds her Catholicism against her out of a feeling of his own inadequacy as husband and provider. More orally fixated, it seems, than his babies, he becomes a slave to the bottle in spite of the fact that liquor makes his ulcer flare. Physically, emotionally, and spiritually the man is a mess. For Cass Kinsolving is a man without faith, and a man without faith cannot produce good art or live a satisfactory life. He recounts to Leverett the time when he was seventeen years old, and about to have his first sexual experience with Vernelle Satterfield, the comely young Jehovah's Witness. His premature ejaculation evokes her telling remark, "The divine spirit just flowed right on out of you." Kinsolving has always remembered that remark and recognizes the truth of it: he has all his life been in search of an Eden that remains out of his reach, and to save his life he needs an infusion of the divine spirit. But he is imprisoned in the house of self, with no one, neither human nor God, coming with the key.

A dream that Kinsolving has in Paris during one of his dark nights of the soul—when he throws Poppy and the children out of the house—provides a clue to the source of his despair and self-loathing. Dreams are especially important in this novel: as sources of information that can partially circumvent the conscious mind with its rationalizations and suppressions, they provide a way for the characters to find out who they really are. Kinsolving dreams that he is incarcerated in the state prison, but he is ignorant of the charge. So heinous is his crime that the other prisoners call for him to be gassed, but still he cannot discover the nature of his deed; in dream terms, perhaps it is unspeakable to him. Clearly, Kinsolving is burdened with a sense of guilt and wants to die because he feels he deserves this fate: hence his self-destructive actions. When three of his children come down with scarlet fever on the train to Toulon, Kinsolving is convinced that he is being punished by God for his sins, that in some deep sense, he, a worthless derelict, has destroyed his own children. While he attributes their eventual recovery to penicillin, Poppy attributes the miracle to God, for she is a woman of tremendous faith, and he thirsts for God with a spiritual need so deep that no man-made potions can slake it.

Kinsolving is exquisitely aware of and sensitive to the suffering he sees around him in Sambuco, where he has fled with his family from Rome. He sees the wretched poverty and misery as stemming from a God not malevolent but inept. Two incidents make an especially deep impression on him. In one, a dog is hit by a bus, its hind parts crushed, yet it struggles to live and has to be put out of its misery. Incredibly, the town doctor's attempts to destroy it with a stick are unsuccessful, so strong is the dog's will to survive and so ineffectual the doctor's strength. Kinsolving flees from the scene, never witnessing its inevitable conclusion, but remembering always the beast's dumb and perpetual agony. In another incident, one of the innumerable, seemingly interchangeable old peasant women, bearing a load of fagots too heavy for her fragile back, lets her burden slip accidentally from her shoulders and struggles painfully to take it on again. The struggle upsets Kinsolving, watching in a drunken stupor from his café table, and he closes his eyes to it, thereby missing the resolution of the problem. These incomplete episodes sink into Kinsolving's consciousness and their salient points combine into one horrendous dream, in which a dog, crushed by a bus, transmogrifies into a scrawny peasant woman hit repeatedly by the bus driver in an attempt to put out of her misery. She shrieks continuously for release from her pain, but the driver succeeds only in instilling more pain. To Kinsolving, the dream symbolizes God's relation to His creations: the human condition is one of pain and misery, but so ridiculously strong is the human will to live that God Himself cannot snuff out this pathetic suffering creature, though not for want of trying.

This bleak vision of the world prompts Kinsolving to attempt suicide by throwing himself off a cliff. In Paris, after his guilt-suffused dream of prison, he had considered killing his whole family with gas, and now he has another dream in which he splits in two and watches his other self step into a shower, turn on the faucets, and release clouds of asphyxiating gas from the nozzles. As in his Paris dream, blacks play a prominent part in the fantasized events, and Kinsolving recognizes that some important and never fully resolved conflict is being played out in his subconscious mind. About half his nightmares since coming to Europe have been connected with blacks, he realizes. The significance of that fact is contained in an incident from Kinsolving's teenage years, which he recounts to Peter Leverett during the visit in Charleston. At the age of fifteen or sixteen, working in a Western Auto store in a backwoods Virginia town, Kinsolving accompanies Lonnie, the assistant manager, to the cabin of a black farmer who has defaulted on his payments for a small radio. While the farmer is out in the fields, Lonnie searches the derelict house and finds the cheap plastic radio hidden under a floorboard. The crack in the casing arouses his fury, and he begins systematically to destroy the farmer's meager possessions. The young Cass looks on with horror, but with excitement too, and not only does he fail to give voice to his disapproval but he also joins in the destruction when commanded. So deep is his guilt at doing what he knows is wrong that Kinsolving puts the incident out of his mind for another fifteen years. It surfaces in Sambuco, however, when Kinsolving's feeling of self-worth is treacherously low, adding to the burden of shame and remorse that he already bears for countless other misdeeds.

No doubt this particular crime against the black man seeks its fitting punishment in the death-in-life existence that Kinsolving leads in thrall to Mason Flagg, subject to verbal abuse and psychological defilement, owned by someone higher in the social order who is morally practically worthless. One of the first things that Poppy Kinsolving tells Peter Leverett when they meet in Sambuco is that Mason Flagg dominates her husband. Cass himself admits, in retrospect, that he became a regular peon to Flagg. The master-slave nature of their relationship is made clear by the humiliating acts Flagg has Kinsolving perform for the entertainment of the Hollywood crew, including a recitation, in slave dialect and to the tune of "Old Black Joe," of a poem about Abraham Lincoln. So desperate is Cass Kinsolving to be owned and treated like dirt, and so desperate is he for the material support provided by Flagg, that he prostitutes even his artistic talent, painting, at Flagg's request, a pornographic picture to add to Flagg's collection. What further bargains the devilish Flagg would like to strike in exchange for Kinsolving's soul are cut short by the climactic events of the story. But one may construe from hints that they concern Cass's becoming a panderer, procuring Francesca Ricci for the degenerate Flagg in order to gain for Francesca's father, Michele, the drug that might save his life.

Mason Flagg fully recognizes the hold that he has over Kinsolving where the Ricci family is concerned. Although Francesca responds warmly only to Cass, it is Mason who has the money to employ her. Whereas only Cass is interested in ministering to the dying Michele, it is Mason who has access to the drugs as well as the money to buy them. Paradoxically, Kinsolving's utter dependence upon Flagg for contact with Francesca and medicine for her father is also a way out of servitude, for in serving the needs of the Ricci family Kinsolving finds a focus for his life and an exit from preoccupation with self. His submission to Mason Flagg gradually and subtly changes in character as Cass himself changes, moving closer to a condition of freedom. This movement does not go unnoticed by Flagg. Out of desperation to retain his "property," Flagg withholds the necessary drug and rapes Francesca. Thinking that Flagg has also murdered Francesca, Cass takes his retribution by bashing in Flagg's head and throwing him off the cliff.

Two years later, when Leverett and Kinsolving recollect these events during the calm South Carolina afternoons, they acknowledge the complexity of the moral situation and the difficulty of affixing blame. Who caused the rape and the murder of Francesca as well as the death of Mason Flagg? Certainly Flagg himself was the evil one, the perpetrator of gross and vile deeds. But as the story unfolds, as layer upon layer is stripped away, one gets to the core of the truth, a simple nugget: neither Peter nor

Cass is without complicity in these crimes. Peter Leverett has
known throughout his adult life that Flagg had the potential to
inflict great harm on women, but he has kept his mouth shut. In
New York he doesn't act on the information given him by Flagg's
wife, Celia, who appears at his doorstep bloody and beaten by
her husband. In Sambuco he doesn't speak up when he sees
Mason strike his mistress, Rosemarie. Not surprisingly, Mason
Flagg says that his mother liked Peter so much precisely because
he kept quiet about what he observed. If Leverett, in these failures to act, abets Mason Flagg in his rape of Francesca, he also
abets Cass Kinsolving in his murder of Flagg. For Leverett is
stone sober and can see perfectly well that Cass is a desperate
man, while Cass himself is too figuratively nearsighted to assess
his situation fully. It lies within Leverett's power to get help for
Cass, and help is near at hand in the person of Hollywood
director Alonzo Cripps. But Leverett does not seize control of
the situation, partially because he himself is confused and guilt-
ridden over the accident with the Italian motorcyclist.

As for Cass Kinsolving, the pattern of his inaction has been
clear from the beginning. He lives off his wife's inheritance,
without the necessity for working. He takes no responsibility for
the pathetic turns of his life, like the loss of that inheritance,
attributing them to the stupidity or venality of others. For a
while, after the illness of his children, Kinsolving swears off
liquor, but he is easily tempted to it again. When the McCabes
take him for all his money during an evening of card playing in
Paris, Kinsolving attributes the turn of events not to his weak-
ness of character but rather to his having "simply been set down
in a situation over which he had utterly no control." In spite of
his genuine love for Francesca, he fails to deflect Mason Flagg's
patently lewd attentions, and his inability to take decisive steps
to protect her contributes directly to her tragedy.

Cass Kinsolving is weighted down into inaction by his bleak
vision of life as symbolized by the peasant woman with her load
of fagots. She has been dealt a burden that she cannot shoulder
without great pain. Cass does not help her to lift her burden, for
he is as repulsed by her as he is by the dog lying crushed on the
street. His "paralyzing death of the soul," as he later terms it,

causes him to see only the nullity of the universe. His horror of nothingness is exceeded only by his horror of *being*, which grows from his failure to acknowledge the value of life. The way out of this hellish existence is provided by Michele Ricci, for complex reasons associated in part with Cass's love for Ricci's daughter and in part with the similarity in Cass's mind between Ricci's hovel and the cabin of the black sharecropper back in Sussex County, Virginia. Helping Ricci in the wretchedness of his poverty is a way of making amends for past actions or inactions, and thus of restoring motivity to the paralyzed soul.

Cass Kinsolving's extreme situation provides the means for two of the other important characters to get out of a disabling preoccupation with self. Peter Leverett's foray with Cass to the Tramonti cottage of Michele Ricci strips him of illusions about what life has to offer. Gone forever is the facile belief in beauty for the taking. A view into the netherworld of Italian life leads Peter Leverett to take charge of Poppy Kinsolving and the children, who are relative strangers to him, when Cass flees their home for a couple of days after killing Mason. Leverett literally puts the house back in order, and thus helps Cass, upon his return, to find a refuge and a haven. By bearing witness to these cataclysmic events, Leverett learns what Kinsolving, too, has learned: that hell is definable as a state of true selfishness. One cannot be sure that Leverett's life has become better because of this lesson: that he becomes a better lawyer, for example, concerned with justice rather than with rules and regulations. But having been tested in the crucible of experience, he has certainly changed, deepened, mellowed. As Kinsolving notes, quoting from *King Lear*, ripeness is all.

So, too, the police corporal, Luigi Migliore, becomes a different man because of the events in Sambuco. As a boy in World War II he sees his younger brother hit and incinerated by a British bomb meant for the Germans, and the experience turns him into a cold, unfeeling man with a burning desire for revenge. Cass's experiences show Luigi the futility of dwelling in the past as well as the incapacitating nature of hatred. His disbelief in God (How could God create a world of such suffering and misery?) is tempered somewhat by the goodness that he sees in

Cass after allowing himself to become as close to Cass as a brother—the brother that he has lost, perhaps. Luigi's view is that life
is a prison, with an unreachable jailer. It is the human lot to be
prisoners on earth with no chance of escape. Yet there is freedom in imprisonment, even if narrowly defined. People may
make choices to find and create joy, to renounce self-pity and
self-consuming guilt, to do good, and to opt for life. If Mason
Flagg's urge toward life was fake and feverish, a yea-saying of
the flesh alone, Luigi's urge toward life is sober, reasoned, and
spiritual. It honors God, the absent jailer, by respecting life in
any form. And it is Cass Kinsolving, with his love for Francesca
and Michele, who shows Luigi that the peasants the policeman
had formerly disparaged and ignored are people rather than
anonymous ciphers.

Because of Luigi's affection for Cass Kinsolving, and belief in
his worth, he tells a lie to the police inspector. Although he
knows that the retarded oaf Saverio was the savage attacker of
Francesca, and Kinsolving the murderer of Flagg, he concocts a
story implicating Flagg in the attack and provides a motive for
murder and apparent suicide. In Luigi's view, true justice lives
"in the heart, locked away from politics and government and
even the law." He releases Cass to a condition of freedom, a
burden that Cass is fearful of taking up since it puts the responsibility for the conduct of life squarely on himself. A true policeman, Luigi acts out of a desire for correction. Fittingly, he is
elevated to sergeant after the case is closed. Whether he will
become a better or worse police officer because of his promotion
remains to be seen. His first act as sergeant is promising, for he
has Saverio put away, a move long rejected by his predecessor,
Pavinello, who therefore must also share in the blame for the
deaths of Francesca Ricci and Mason Flagg.

Luigi Migliore's lie to the police captain is in stark contrast to
Mason Flagg's lifetime of lies. Mason meticulously differentiates
between lies and the jazzy extravaganzas that he tells, meant
only to entertain. But his entire life is an illusion, and he deals in
illusions only as a way of avoiding such realities as his lack of
talent and his inability to love. Cass Kinsolving also deals in
illusions, but, like Luigi's, they are lies in the service of life. In

order to soothe the dying Michele, Cass tells him stories about America, which Michele has always wanted to visit. He embroiders his stories outrageously, presenting a fantasy vision of the United States that entertains and momentarily distracts a man in pain. Wonder of wonders, these tales help to heal the teller, pulling him back to his native country where the process of self-regeneration must be continued.

Kinsolving's attitude toward America is ambivalent. He flees the "soft-headed, baby-faced, predigested, cellophane wrapped, doomed, beauty-hating land." Styron suggests that Flagg, like the flag, represents America; more specifically, like Emilio Narduzzo's six-fold Old Glory, waving over his palatial villa, Flagg represents American materialism. Kinsolving denigrates the trappings of the good life that Flagg provides, yet he simultaneously avails himself of Mason's liquor, bananas, and milk. He recognizes that the wonder drug he needs for Michele is available only because of American technology. Above all, Kinsolving misses the country scenes of his childhood: the sight and smell of pine trees, the sound of blacks singing in the churches in the grove, or of a freight-train whistle. Of these sights and sounds is he made: they define him. In fleeing his country, Cass Kinsolving flees himself and his responsibility for his backwoods crime against the Virginia farmer. In returning to his country, Kinsolving makes proper use of the past, coming to terms with his origins and with his identity as a journeyman cartoonist from Lake Waccamaw, North Carolina. He takes up cartooning in Charleston—an American art form, Cass surmises—and turns his poisonous thoughts about the United States into effective political cartoons reprinted in the New York *Times*. It's not the life he dreamed of, it's a life of compromises, but it's a life nonetheless, and not the death-in-life of his previous existence.

Cass Kinsolving has undergone the test by fire that Peter Leverett's father had prescribed for all Americans, to turn them from ciphers (a favorite Styron word) into human beings. The novel has elements of a Greek tragedy, in which the theme of crime and punishment is paramount. Styron points the reader toward Greek tragedy in several ways. Peter Leverett learns of the deaths of Mason Flagg and Francesca Ricci from the hotel owner, Fausto Windgasser, who laments that it's an "overpowering twagedy, my God. It's like the Gweeks, I tell you, but far worse!" Although Windgasser (whose name says it all) is more concerned with the effect of these events on tourism in Sambuco than he is with their moral or spiritual dimension, his fluttery pronouncement is one of the many ways by which Styron draws the reader's attention to "the Greeks." Cass Kinsolving continually spouts Sophocles in his drunken states and often can be found reading *Complete Greek Drama* in European cafés. However, in his letter to Leverett early on in the novel, after Leverett reinitiates contact between them, Kinsolving notes that it is easier to read Sophocles sober than drunk. The full meaning of Sophocles for Styron, as for Kinsolving, is gradually revealed over the course of the book.

Kinsolving suffers some sort of mental breakdown while in the marines and undergoes treatment in the form of extensive conversations with a military psychiatrist named Slotkin. Slotkin gives Kinsolving the Sophoclean plays to read, and the two of them—one a Jewish physician from Brookline, Massachusetts, the other a Southern Methodist from rural North Carolina, with only two years of high school—discuss the ethical as well as the psychoanalytical implications of Kinsolving's illness by reference to Sophocles and his characters, particularly Oedipus. Kinsolving's quoting from Oedipus's lines about wishing for death elicits Slotkin's rejoinder that the Greeks tried, in spite of repeated failure, to free people into the condition of love. Kinsolving keeps Slotkin's words in mind in the midst of his alcoholic fogs and psychological distresses. When he is in the depths of despair, in slavery to Mason Flagg, he calls upon Slotkin, his "old father, old rabbi," for guidance. Slotkin remains throughout the novel, as throughout Kinsolving's life, as an unseen but very real father figure, advocating wisdom from suffering and resistance to the death urge. Oedipus himself is a guide for Kinsolving, for the grand king, burdened with guilt, does not kill himself, but rather lives on into old age. In *Oedipus at Colonus*, from which Kinsolving often quotes, Oedipus begins as a dependent, blind old man and grows into true kingly stature, uncrushed by adversity. He retains, and in fact asserts, his dignity as a human being. Sophocles cannot justify God's ways to man, but he does justify man's ways to man. Styron's intent is to do the same.

Cass Kinsolving exhorts Alonzo Cripps to cast out his crew of Hollywood tinsel types and to put on a very different kind of theater in this modern world: "We'll pull a Prometheus on 'em. We'll bring back tragedy to the land of the Pepsi-Cola and the peanut brittle and the Modess Because." This, we remember, had been the prescription for the soul's ills made by Alfred Leverett, another father guide. The reference to pulling a Prometheus—that is, to bringing fire to humankind—ties in with the title of the novel and with its epigraph from a seventeenth-century sermon by John Donne. The sermon uses the metaphor of the body as a house in which the soul resides. A miserable, damned creature, remote from God, has its soul hidden deep within the recesses. But God makes a determined effort to reach and then to release the soul, if necessary with flames of torment. The pain of such purgatorial cleansing is pleasure compared to the prospect of eternal seclusion from God. In Styron's novel, Mason Flagg's palazzo, dedicated to the pursuit of fleshly pleasures, is equivalent to the body. A bird, traditionally emblematic of the soul or the holy spirit, struggles to escape from the enclosed courtyard. Only when Cass Kinsolving, an underground man who is living in the basement of the palazzo, struggles to the summit and casts off Mason Flagg is a flock of birds seen ascending to the heavens.

Styron does not press the religious nature of these symbols, but it is always implied, especially because of the structure of the novel as a kind of Dante's *Inferno* and the characterization of Poppy Kinsolving, Cass's wife, as a Beatrice figure. Dante is guided through hell by Virgil and led out of hell by Beatrice. If, in *Set This House on Fire*, Peter Leverett plays Virgil to Cass's Dante, then Poppy plays Beatrice. Poppy is barely a woman of this world: ethereal, almost bodiless, she cannot keep rotting food off the floor or deal with financial affairs, but she is animated and energized by her belief in God. A kind of angelic or saintly spirit, who seems most of the time to be dressed in a white slip, Poppy floats on top of the scum, kept buoyant by her faith. Her sticking it out with Cass, a man who lives off her, berates her, throws her out of the house, and thinks of killing her, appears foolish by any standards of reason or intellect; but these are not Poppy's standards. Ultimately she is vindicated: Cass does turn out to be a worthy, even superior, individual, who chooses being over nothingness and sets out to be whatever it is he can be, for as long as he can be it.

The epilogue to *Set This House on Fire* provides distance from the cataclysmic events of the novel and adds a comic dimension to the tragedy, setting the inferno in a larger context and making the work a *Divine Comedy* of sorts. Cass Kinsolving writes to Peter some months after their extended visit that he is quite busy with his painting classes and that Poppy is expecting another baby. This is no Paradise, but it is paradisal compared to the life Cass knew previously. If Charleston, South Carolina, is no Florence, Italy, at least it provides him with gainful and even satisfying employment. If Poppy is not voluptuous Francesca Ricci, she is nonetheless Cass's wife, whom he loves, and her pregnancy is both a sign of that love and hope for the future. Cass's letter makes reference to something that Peter Leverett has mentioned in his own letter—that Peter has put his life in order, and has found himself a sweetheart. Both men, apparently, have shored up their foundations after extracting the meaning of those events in Sambuco. Both have experienced a kind of rebirth.

The epilogue reveals another resurrection. Luciano di Lieto, the unfortunate victim of a collision with Leverett's sport's car, has been languishing in a coma ever since the accident at least two years earlier. Dutifully, Peter Leverett has been sending a regular check for his care to the nuns in the nursing home in Italy. Now, a month after the arrival of Cass's letter, Peter receives word from the good sister that Luciano has miraculously recovered, risen like a phoenix from the ashes of his destruction. A postscript to the letter updates the medical report, saying that Luciano was soon readmitted to the hospital with a broken collarbone after falling down a flight of stairs. But he is smiling, alert, and even affianced! So durable is the human spirit, so infinite the capacity for achieving a second chance. The novel ends on a note of affirmation—hard won and tentative, but an affirmation nonetheless. Suffering is not a good in itself, nor does it necessarily lead to grace, but after suffering one might learn what is truly of value, and might come to see that life itself is good. Phoenix-like, one can rise from the ashes of affliction and despair, over and over again.

5

~~~~~~

Styron's Farewell to Arms: Writings on the Military

War, the ultimate adventure, the ordinary man's most convenient means of escaping from the ordinary.

—Styron quoting Philip Caputo's *A Rumor of War*, in "A Farewell to Arms," *New York Review of Books*, June 23, 1977

William Styron was attracted to the military profession for the first seventeen years of his life. The attraction was as much a part of his birthright as his Southernness, for the military tradition grew thick on both sides of his family tree, symbolized by the silver-handled sword presented to a great-great-uncle for valiant service in the Mexican-American War. Styron's paternal grandfather fought for the Confederacy in the Civil War; his maternal uncle, a West Pointer, was a boyhood friend of George C. Marshall, the noted World War II commander. In Styron's youth, during the 1930s, dinner-table talk of battles long past or recent was accompanied by the bustle of martial affairs in the Tidewater environs, as the nation geared for war. The new Flying Fortresses droned from Langley Field, joined by the racket from navy fighter planes out of the Norfolk air station as well as by the buzz of activity at the Newport News shipyard, biggest in the country, where Styron's father worked. "In this environment," Styron says, "and with my deeply belligerent heritage, there is little wonder that the Service came to figure prominently in my disposition."[1]

At the age of seventeen Styron joined the Marine Corps, serving altogether for more than three years in two different wars, as both an enlisted man and an officer. Although his initial infatuation with the military calling in general, and with the marines in particular, quickly cooled, Styron's interest in the military has never diminished. War and the men who wage it figure importantly in most of Styron's works. Except for *The Confessions of Nat Turner*, set in the nineteenth century, all of Styron's major novels deal to some extent with the wars in which the writer himself participated. As already noted, World War II and the bombing of Nagasaki form the global background against which the Loftis family plays out its domestic tragedy in *Lie Down in Darkness*. Cass Kinsolving's mental breakdown during World War II brings him into the care of a military psychiatrist, Slotkin, whose values Kinsolving will later adopt as a standard bearer in more personal battles. The Nazi persecution of non-Aryans is the horror that forces Sophie's choice in the novel of that name, and reinforces the dark vision of life that will forever color Stingo's art.

Three of Styron's major works of fiction are focused centrally on the military: *The Long March, In the Clap Shack*, and *The Way of the Warrior* (in progress). In the first two of these, published twenty years apart, war is emblematic of human existence: its bureaucracy and impersonality represent all institutions; the isolation and fear of its combatants are the primary conditions of modern life.

Lieutenant Culver of *The Long March*, like many of Styron's protagonists, looks nostalgically from a chaotic present into an Edenic past. He has left behind a law practice, his family, and the strains of Haydn, Bach, and Mozart reverberating through peaceful Sunday afternoons in New York City. Now his companions are his fellow marine reservists in the Headquarters and Service Company in rural North Carolina, his comfortable existence exchanged for endless maneuvers during frigid nights and torrid days in training for possible combat in Korea. The surrealistic pursuit of an imaginary enemy, the relentless exhaustion, and the isolation from all ordinary endeavors fill Culver with confusion, apprehension, and dismay. This sense of disorder and chaos is replicated in Styron's narrative technique, which substitutes flashback within flashback for a chronological sequence of events. The first two chapters of the novella proceed by means of flashbacks to present the central event of the novel: not the long march of the title, as one might suspect, but the event that causes the march to take on its utmost meaning—that is, the accidental short firing of rounds that kills eight soldiers in the next battalion.

Chapter 1 begins at the scene of carnage, with the bodies strewn about and Lieutenant Culver off to the side vomiting at the sight. The rest of the chapter relates, through flashback, how Culver came to be in marine camp, and what he left behind. Chapter 2 starts at the moment when Culver and his company are eating lunch in a command post and hear the explosion off in the distance. The rest of the chapter focuses on the order for the long march and introduces the antagonists, Colonel Templeton and Captain Mannix, whose personalities are adumbrated mainly through flashbacks. Chapters 3 and 4 deal with the march itself—a thirty-six mile, thirteen-hour trek at two-and-one-half miles per hour. No lengthy flashbacks occur here, for the agonizing present blots out thoughts of anything but blind, dogged survival. Yet even here, near the beginnings of chapters 3 and 4, the explosion and deaths figure prominently, hovering at the fringes of Culver's consciousness and accounting, in Culver's mind, for Captain Mannix's moody behavior. The final chapter, a postmarch coda, also begins with mention of the dead marines. They function as a leitmotiv in this story, a picture returning to the main characters' minds, as to the reader's, "with the unshakable regularity of a scrap of music."

The novella, then, focuses on a tragedy: the slaughter of eight young marines through what would come to be known in the Vietnam War as "friendly fire." Because of this accident, and because of the stateside setting in a noncombat situation, the characters wonder about the identity of their real enemy. Who is the invisible aggressor whom the reservists relentlessly stalk, against whom the commanding officers ceaselessly warn? The state of exhaustion in which the reservists perpetually exist, for they are woefully out of shape, softened by the good life back home, makes the answer to that question unclear to Culver, who plays the role of Everyman in this story. Through Culver's eyes the reader views the man who plays the role of tragic hero, the platoon leader Al Mannix. A man of mythological proportions, compared implicitly to Atlas and to Christ, Mannix identifies the enemy as the military system itself and proceeds to knock his head against the nature of things in an effort to beat the system. Through this effort, which is ridiculous and even aberrant by standards of sanity and propriety, Mannix wrests control over his life from the powers-that-be and asserts the humanity of the boys who died as well as of the reservists he leads.

The story of Mannix's perverse rebellion cannot be understood unless the nature of military service as Styron views it is first delineated. Styron does not regard the military as an inherently evil profession, but, ever suspicious of institutions, he considers it to be a bureaucracy that stifles individuality. The reservists in H & S Company must all be treated alike, as marines; all-important is the esprit de corps that bonds the many into the one. In this sense the men are nonentities rather than fully realized human beings. Sergeant O'Leary, a marine regular, is said to be grafted onto the military system like a piece of skin, and therefore molded into the image of marine. The reader is reminded that the outcome may be similarly dehumanizing: the eight dead marines look as if they've been sprayed from a hose, turned into mere shreds of skin and bone that seem never to have been alive at all. Because the reservists have known freedom, they are especially resistant to the authority wielded by Colonel Templeton and his officers.

This authority manifests itself most forcefully in Colonel Templeton's order for a thirty-six-mile march that will toughen the reservists, prepare them for actual combat, and make them more like the regulars. The order and the subsequent march fill Culver and Mannix with revulsion and fear, not merely because they doubt their ability to withstand the heat and the pain, but, more importantly, because they are loath to relinquish their free

will: "How stupid to think they had ever made their own philos-
ophy; it was as puny as a house of straw, and at this moment—
by the noise in their brains of those words, *you will*—it was being
blasted to the winds like dust. They were as helpless as children." The military reduces the fighting men to the state of children, belittled as it were, with the commanding officers as powerful parental figures determining the course of their charges'
lives—fathers, maybe, or even priests, invested with a quasi-
divine authority. Culver, calling "Bundle Able" on the radio at
Colonel Templeton's request, feels "juvenile and absurd, as if he
were reciting Mother Goose." Mannix has only contempt for this
code language of military communication that replaces ordinary
conversation with boy-scout passwords. Major Lawrence, subservient to the colonel, looks to Culver like a five-year-old child,
and speaks to the colonel in the third person as if Templeton
were an imperial ruler and the major his subject.

Other figures of speech, more emotionally charged than the
references to children, hint at the odious status of the soldiers.
Captain Mannix is compared at one point to a shackled slave,
and at another to a chain-gang convict. By these means Styron
conveys the idea that the military imprisons the individual and
subordinates him to the system. Quite simply, the marines are
not free men. Mannix despises Templeton for the authority that
Templeton wields, not only because authority is anathema to
this rebellious individual, but also because Mannix is all too
aware of the fallibility of those who wield the power. The accidental misfiring of the missiles and the resultant death of the
eight young marines may well have been caused by the decision
to use old shells stored on Guam since 1945. Such disregard for
the consequences of decisions bespeaks a lack of connection
between those who give the orders and those who do the fighting. This lack of communication between commander and commanded—indeed, between men in general—is symbolized by
the incident that Mannix relates to Culver from his buck-ser-
geant days during World War II. Pinned down in his shell hole
under heavy fire from the Japanese, Mannix screams desperately
into the telephone for assistance. Each time he hollers for aid he

gets hit by another piece of shrapnel. Just before losing consciousness he notices that the telephone wires have all along
been severed. There has been no lifeline between him and others. Instead, he is on his own, to succeed or fail on his own
powers along with the luck of the draw. Even the radio over
which Lieutenant Culver tries to make contact with Able Company emits only a banshee wail of signals, "like the cries of
souls in the anguish of hell." No call to that company gets
through, so isolated and uprooted are these men. To Styron, this
situation of being cut off is the human condition. Alienated from
his God, estranged from his fellows, the individual cannot count
for aid and comfort on the ministrations of anyone else; he had
best rely on himself.

And so, because the dead soldiers could not take control
over their lives, Captain Al Mannix takes control over his. He
does not opt out of the marines, for he has made his commitment. (This is, after all, the Korean War in the conformist 1950s;
the next war, in the next decade, would tell a different tale.)
Rather, he chooses to exert the full force of his individuality
within the strict parameters of the military system. If Colonel
Templeton, nicknamed Old Rocky because of his obdurate nature, can order thirty-year-old, out-of-shape reservists to march
for thirteen hours, then Captain Mannix can find his own way of
being an immovable object. He finds it in a rebellion in reverse—
that is, in seeing the march through to its end and exhorting his
company to do the same. Mannix accomplishes this task under
especially grievous conditions; added to the fatigue and heat suffered by all the marchers is the discomfort of a nail sticking up
from his boot into his foot, resisting his best efforts at removal.
Marching for Mannix becomes a true torture, and thus a true test
of his human capacity to endure. The nail and the injury it
causes provide Mannix with an escape from the forced march if
he wants it: Templeton commands him to ride in on the truck.
But Mannix chooses to obey the first command, to march, rather
than the second one, and thereby enacts his perverse rebellion.
This "one personal insurrection" cannot hope to accomplish
much good. Indeed, it turns Mannix into a taskmaster, bullying
his men into completing the march with him. It injures his foot

and makes every step a crucifixion. It gets him confined to quarters, and perhaps even courtmartialed, after cursing the colonel. But if this insurrection is absurd it is not therefore without value. In fact, it does get Mannix from point A to point B *on his own terms*. And he does indeed carry some of his company on his back, Atlas-like, completing his superhuman task almost like a god rather than a man, elevating his men in spite of themselves. By refusing to drop out or to let them drop out (though two-thirds of them eventually do), he asserts the dignity and worth of human life and thereby wrests control for the individual from dominating outside forces. Though comical, caricatural, and even bizarre, Mannix's gesture attests to the durability of the human spirit.

If Mannix is not necessarily to be considered a fool, is he therefore to be considered a hero? Styron thinks so. In the midst of senseless slaughter and a senseless, seemingly endless march, in a war presaging the "forceless, soulless, pushbutton wars of the future,"[2] one indefatigable man with an indomitable will imprints his features on the action. By so doing he fights the battle of the luckless marine whose "face had been blasted out of sight" while he waited for his lunch. Templeton's own face is likened to a mannequin's, betokening his lack of humanity, and the loaded pearl-handled revolver he wears on his hip is a sign of the military's potential to turn humans into inert matter in one moment, as the short rounds did to the men on the chow line; the forks and spoons of the dead soldiers were turned into "pathetic metal flowers," completing the inhuman and unnatural picture. Mannix is ennobled by his suffering, which personalizes the impersonal order to march and humanizes the dehumanizing task of carrying out this order. His rebellion therefore sets the world in order, if only temporarily. The reader recalls the episode related by Mannix to Culver about his most harrowing experience during World War II. On a spree out of boot camp, on the tenth floor of a hotel in San Francisco, Mannix had been suspended for several long minutes naked and upside down from the window by a couple of drunken marines. The utter helplessness and disorientation of the situation were too horrible for bearing. Human existence, Styron implies, is often an upside-down view into the abyss. Any attempt to set the world rightside up and to provide something to hold onto is a laudable, even heroic task.

Throughout the novella Styron draws attention to Mannix's body. Whereas the other characters are clothed and protected, Mannix is often pictured naked and vulnerable. One is aware of his fleshiness, his mortality; he is massive and hairy, larger than life. Mannix points out to Culver the many scars covering his entire body. He seems almost a mass of wounds, and he shows them off not proudly but matter-of-factly, as if to say, this is what it means to be alive. He is wounded and suffers because he dares. His emotions are not controlled, his responses are not programmed. Mannix is a man, not a machine.

The final scene of the novella drives home this point. Mannix has showered after his long march and proceeds down the hall draped only in a towel, clutching the wall for support and dragging his maimed leg behind him. His suffering is described as gigantic, befitting this man's physical and spiritual proportions. He meets the black maid, whose sympathy for his condition is immediate and genuine as she asks him if he is in pain. He communicates a complex set of emotions to the maid without jargon, without lies, almost even without words. As he struggles to remain upright the towel falls away, and for one last moment he stands naked and exposed, his body a mass of scars. Tomorrow Mannix may be court-martialed, his world turned topsy turvy again. But for today he has made it through, vulnerable and suffering as ever, but still standing. And that, at least for now, is triumph enough.

Styron's play, *In the Clap Shack*, deals with similar themes in a very different kind of setting. Whereas *The Long March* conveys a sense of dizzying, disorienting space, *In the Clap Shack* transmits a paralyzing sense of claustrophobia. The action takes place on a urological ward of a navy hospital in the southern United States during the summer of 1943. According to the stage directions, the scene is dominated by two rows of nine beds each, feet facing a central aisle. The men in this ward are incarcerated primarily for venereal diseases; of the fifteen patients, only four are there for other reasons. At stage left is the chief urologist's office, from which the doctor "rules the ward." A radio plays "Don't Fence Me In" as an appropriate commentary on the feelings of the imprisoned marines. Styron has remarked in another context of the "sharp sense of imprisonment" evoked by the lyrics of popular songs. "When played in a martial setting, popular songs have a way of heightening one's mood of isolation; dealing with peaceable pursuits like ball games and courtship, they tend to sadden, and to mock one's ears. In the Second World War, this song for me was 'Don't Fence Me In'."[3]

Into this military establishment Styron places marines with a variety of ethnic or racial identifications: a Pole, an Italian, an Irishman, a Jew, a black. This feature, common to war fiction and movies, makes of the urological ward a democratic melting pot much like the country itself. It also gives Styron an opportunity to explore the relations between different groups of Americans, especially those between Christian and Jew, white and black. The main character, Wally Magruder, is an eighteen-year-old raw recruit from Virginia, a kind of Protestant Everyman. Although he has been placed in the ward for suspected syphilis he seems virginal and childlike, and his naive views of life are played off against the well-formed prejudices and habits of the older men. The oldest inhabitant of the ward is Schwartz, a northern Jew with renal tuberculosis. Magruder holds most of his conversations with Schwartz and with Lorenzo Clark, a southern black who is dying of kidney disease. The other marines, with names like Stancik, Dadario, and McDaniel, remain, for the most part, in the background of the play.

Terminal illness has not sweetened the dispositions nor softened the prejudices of these men. Schwartz calls Clark an evil *Schwarze* and a nigger; his own name, also meaning *black*, is never spoken by Clark, who prefers to call him Jew-boy. Clark falsely accuses Schwartz of stealing Magruder's wallet, and Schwartz turns on Magruder with the epithet, "dirty, degenerate *Southern-born cracker*." When Magruder's wallet is returned by the hospital laundry, Magruder pounces on the "black no good son of a bitch." And so it goes, with each man denigrating the other, their illnesses making them even more vulnerable and sensitive to insults and slights. That both Schwartz and Clark are members of minority groups—that they are essentially *Schwarzes* in the view of society—does not bring them together in mutual understanding. Schwartz prides himself on his tolerance for others, which he buttresses by consulting Rabbi Max Weinberg's *Tolerance for Others, or How to Develop Human Compassion*, but only at Clark's death does Schwartz attempt communication. It is a matter of too little too late, however, mixed with a heavy dose of Clark's implacable hatred. The black man dies pitifully alone.

The attitudes of the three "healthy" characters—Budwinkle, the hospital commandant; Glanz, the chief urologist; and Lineweaver, the chief nurse—are sickest of all. Schwartz is treated with bemused tolerance, like a zoological curiosity or exotic species. But Clark is another case. Glanz gives thanks to God that granuloma, an exceptionally virulent disease, is confined almost exclusively to blacks, a sentiment with which Budwinkle tacitly agrees. Lineweaver banters with Clark about barbecued spareribs and "jungle bunnies." Clearly Clark dies as he has lived, singularly isolated from the group of very disparate whites.

Magruder is isolated too, on the basis of his misdiagnosed syphilis. In a "clap shack," or gonorrhea ward, the syphilitic bears the mark of Cain. Indeed, Magruder is forced to wear a robe with a yellow S, and to use separate facilities. In the World War II setting the brand has special meaning that escapes neither Magruder nor Schwartz. Magruder's kinship with Clark on this basis of dislike and exclusion is another, more subtle comparison. But on the ward as in real life, a similarity of position in society does not ensure solidarity among the oppressed. Clark, in his dying, has no use for rapprochement. To the contrary, he continually harps on Magruder's illness, never letting him forget the "spiralkeets" that are eating him up inside. Schwartz, on the other hand, makes a daring move in Magruder's behalf. The men on the ward are imprisoned in their ignorance; the doctor's power and authority are based to a large extent on their privileged knowledge of disease. Therefore, recognizing Magruder's complete helplessness and resolving to aid him, Schwartz borrows one of Glanz's medical textbooks so that they can understand more about syphilis. The move is not without great risk, including the possibility of ten years in the Portsmouth brig if Schwartz is caught. But Schwartz shows himself to be a daring fighter in the war that these men are waging—not against disease only, but against authority and bureaucracy as represented by Glanz and Budwinkle.

Captain Budwinkle sets the tone for the hospital ward that he serves as commandant. According to the stage directions, he is "imperious, patrician of carriage, aloof and proud," decorated with medals and ribbons—the image of "a Hollywood version of a Navy captain." His speech reinforces his clichéd appearance, for he couches everyday language in naval terms. Visiting the hospital to assess the venereal-disease situation, Budwinkle remarks that he's there to get "a clear view from the poop deck . . . so we can navigate the rocks and shoals." His words continually reveal a military point of view, with an emphasis on manliness and ethnocentrism that extends to all areas of his life. He dismisses the British as homosexuals in contrast to Americans, an attitude the audience must deride, having watched the effeminate and probably homosexual Lineweaver. The only British poet admired by Budwinkle is Rudyard Kipling, for Kipling speaks out for country, obedience, and duty.

Styron openly characterizes Budwinkle as a machine rather than a human. The captain delights in the technological gains of warfare, such as the invention of the wire recorder. Dr. Glanz knows that to interest his commandant in the activities of the post, and to cause him to report favorably on the chief urologist, he need only point to the ways that machines take primacy in the daily operation of the hospital. Thus, he steers Budwinkle away from the ward and into the brand-new, up-to-date laboratory. The faith in machines that both Budwinkle and Glanz possess leads them to overvalue gadgetry and to undervalue human emotions. As they converse about Kraft-Stebel monoprecipitators and Banghart twin-speed pressure pumps, a deathly ill marine goes into crisis in the background. Neither Budwinkle nor

Glanz interrupts the conversation to attend to the noise and flurry of activity. Keeping the ward shipshape and using the newest equipment are the primary goals of the administrator and the physician. The patients seem to be nothing but statistics, experimental material on which to apply the pumps and precipitators.

Budwinkle and Glanz rely for their responses on truth as narrowly defined by the military code or the scientific test. Because Wally Magruder's Kahn and Wasserman tests are extremely elevated they assume that Magruder has syphilis. No leap of imagination explores other possibilities, no leap of empathy bridges the gap between the "healthy" and the "sick." When Glanz awakens Magruder to the probability that he has infected his girl Ann with syphilis, neither he nor the captain can understand why Magruder bursts into tears. Magruder's crying even disgusts Budwinkle, for it is to him a sign of effeminacy. Budwinkle and Glanz command Magruder to stop crying, but Magruder is too human to do so. He can't be switched off like a wireless recorder.

Magruder's forgetting to call the bathroom the "head" reveals his lack of comfort with military lingo and, even more, his lack of comfort with military ways. Viewed by Glanz, Budwinkle, and Lineweaver as a king of debauchery, Magruder is instead a wistful, innocent boy who can't understand how this world has suddenly been turned upside-down, and who can't figure out what to do about it. Forcibly removed from fighting the Japanese, thrust into a kind of prison and branded as unfit, Magruder must fight a war against different enemies—first, the invisible spirochetes he is told are destroying him from within, and then Dr. Glanz, the man who is systematically destroying him from without.

Indeed, Glanz is Magruder's nemesis and mirror opposite. If Magruder's heroes are poets like T. S. Eliot and Wallace Stevens, Glanz worships the hero of American industrialism, Henry Ford, along with the creator par excellence of military-marching music, John Philip Sousa, and Rudolph Wachter, the father of bladder surgery, all manly men. According to the stage directions, Dr. Glanz's "every gesture bespeaks obedience to duty and authority." Always anxious to build up his own dignity and importance, Glanz tends to speak in the imperial "we," as if he were a veritable platoon of men. By referring to himself in the third person he puts up a roadblock in communication and simultaneously submerges his personality—the "I"—in a persona. He also magnifies his presence in the sight of his patients and thereby inspires their obedience, as if he were a king.[4] His status as physician already puts him one up on the patients, for he bears a quasi-divine status on the basis of what he knows and what they need. Magruder is especially vulnerable to his feelings of inadequacy and need because he recognizes a streak of hypochondria in himself and has joined the marines in order to become tough. Now he's being told by a doctor that he's very sick indeed, and the combined authority of the medical and military professions seems too much for Magruder to combat.

Because they suffer from venereal disease, most of the patients are subject to a great deal of verbal abuse from Dr. Glanz (how cunningly Styron names him, in light of these illnesses). Glanz regards himself as standard bearer in the war against VD. His moralistic, holier-than-thou attitude creates difficulties for him in living up to the Hippocratic oath, for he believes that the advent of penicillin, a drug that promises to treat most venereal cases effectively, will threaten to release men to fulfill their basest needs. To Styron, both Glanz and Budwinkle have their values backwards, as Budwinkle makes clear when he remarks that "America has a war to wage, but it sure as hell will lose the shooting match if its fighting men persist in waging that war not on the beaches but between the bedsheets." A later era (the one in which Styron created his play) would include the display of bumper stickers reading "make love, not war," which is precisely Styron's implicitly voiced sentiment in this work.[5]

The marines' joy in sex is unbridled. One of them boasts, wishfully no doubt, of intercourse from the age of eight, and makes a list of sixty women whom he has known sexually in the intervening sixteen years. When this marine, Stancik, is released from the hospital, his gonorrhea cured, he promptly makes his plans to "shack up" as soon as possible. That remark elicits a sarcastic rejoinder from Lineweaver: "You're *stupefying*, a real tribute to the life force or something." Of course, the audience has learned to identify Lineweaver with the ruling class and to invert his remarks in order to get at the truth as Styron sees it. Although Lineweaver is not far enough removed from the men to have had his milk of human kindness totally depleted, he is nonetheless a taskmaster who takes perverse pleasure in over-seeing the masturbatory daily ritual that the men must go through for his inspection, to see if treatment is taking effect. In contrast to Lineweaver's condemnatory and smirking attitude, Stancik's attitude toward sex as desirable and even life-enhanc-ing is healthy and sane.

In the course of the play, Dr. Glanz reveals himself as less a urologist than a sexologist, and less a sexologist than a pornogra-pher. On his wireless recorder he takes detailed testimony about the marines' sexual behavior, explaining that the patient's sexual profile is often the key to a successful diagnosis. Glanz believes that the machine has the power to force the truth out of the men, since it can reiterate their words for repeated and intense scruti-ny. Because Glanz is a physician, and a military physician to boot, Magruder reveals the most intimate facts about his sexual relationships. He is so desperately afraid of where he knows syphilis can lead that he grasps at the very weak straw held out by Glanz: "We may be able to try to save your life." Glanz plans these profiles as if they were military engagements, with "Over-views" and "Blitz" phases. In the "Overview" of Magruder's sexual history, Glanz and Budwinkle clearly condemn sex out-side of marriage, calling it fornication, carnal connection, and poisonous business. In contrast, Magruder's attitude toward sex with Ann is poetic and even religious. He has been able to un-derstand and to forgive his one momentary lapse of fidelity to Ann, explaining his sex with a cotton-mill worker on the basis of Ann's absence, Mrs. Yancey's availability, and too much beer. Even more, he believes that Ann would have understood it. Glanz is plainly disturbed by Magruder's lack of guilt and suc-ceeds in whipping some up by reminding the patient that if Ann was a virgin the disease had to be picked up from Mrs. Yancey, and no doubt was transmitted to Ann at a later date. This accusation drives Magruder to tears and then to despair. Sex with Ann had been magnificent, with Mrs. Yancey comical. But until his incarceration in the charnel house, as Magruder calls the hospital ward, sex had never been loathsome.

Session two of Magruder's sexual profile is Glanz's "Blitz" phase, in which the patient gives the moment-by-moment description of the sex act, or an anatomy of intercourse. The audience does not see this interview actually being conducted. Instead, at the end of the play Magruder is seen preparing to enter Dr. Glanz's office after learning that his positive Wasserman was caused by a case of trench mouth rather than syphilis. Poised at the entrance to the office, Magruder overhears Glanz listening to the tape of the session. The stage directions describe the expression on Glanz's face as "sensual, flushed, unabashedly erotic." Clearly, Glanz is getting perverse sexual pleasure from Magruder's recitations; the wireless recorder provides him with a technological substitute for real human emotions, and his authority commands the data he craves. As a stern moralist Dr. Glanz is a poseur, as a healer a fraud. The sight of Glanz hunched over the machine (getting to the crotch of the matter, as he sniggeringly puts it) would be funny if the man were not so dangerous.

Comic elements do abound in *In the Clap Shack*. The basic situation of the play is absurd, even bizarre: incarceration in a venereal-disease ward for nothing more than trench mouth. The men in authority are caricatures—Budwinkle and Glanz relate to each other like members of a vaudeville team—and the actions ridiculous. (Done in pantomime, the "short-arm inspection" is especially funny.) Underlying these comic features is a note of menace. In the hellish pesthole presented by Styron, the healthy are sick, the physically fit are morally and psychologically deformed, the ruling class is inferior to the ruled, and the healer marshals the forces of death rather than those of life. Things are turned topsy-turvy, and the world seen upside down is surrealistic. The patients are not so much human beings as they are house pets, which Styron suggests by having Schwartz reading

How to Manage a Pet Shop. Indeed, Schwartz dreams one night that all the pets in his store are uncaged and running free. There are only two modes of escape from Styron's figurative pet shop—through death or rebellion.

Lorenzo Clark lies down in the darkness of despair and death. Magruder, saved from the same fate by a true diagnosis of his illness, makes a final effort to set things right. At the close of the play, Magruder can no longer tolerate Glanz, not so much because Glanz has pried into the innermost private core of Magruder's life but rather because he has failed at a very human task—instilling hope in the face of despair. Glanz weakly explains that the scientific tools of medicine are not infallible, a fact he had not bothered to announce previously. He continues to assert the doctor's duty not to raise false expectations, though the expectation was true in Magruder's case. And he hides as always behind the imperial "we" of his authority, brooking no questioning from a subordinate. Magruder, however, refuses to remain docile a moment longer. Becoming irate and aggressive at Glanz's feeble excuses, Magruder first brandishes a chair and then pins Glanz to the wall by the neck. As a result of these actions, he faces imprisonment in the Portsmouth brig and a court-martial from the service, but his assault on a superior officer (superior in only a technical sense) has set Magruder free. Like a chorus commenting on the action, the radio in the background announces General MacArthur's victories in the South Pacific. So, too, Wally Magruder has won a war. The spoils of battle are his integrity and his manhood.

Styron has produced many other pieces on the subject of military service. An early portion of his as-yet-uncompleted novel *The Way of the Warrior* appeared as "Marriott, the Marine" in the early 1970s, and it contains many of the elements of *In the Clap Shack*, written approximately at the same time, as well as of the earlier *The Long March*. The story is set in the same period as the novella, the early 1950s, and tells of a marine reservist somewhat like Culver and very much like Styron, called back to active duty to serve in the Korean War. A reservist in a world of regulars, the narrator of the story, like his creator, resents being wrested away from his peacetime life, in which he is about to publish a first novel. The war mentality is alien to him, and the limits to his freedom repugnant. "My emotions," the narrator says, "must have been very close to those of an ex-convict who has savored the sweet taste of liberty only to find himself once more a transgressor at the prison gates." At the marine camp the narrator is surprised to find that the battalion commander, Paul Marriott, is an erudite and cultured gentleman with a flair for literary criticism and witty conversation, a man as comfortable with the amenities of peacetime living as with the exigencies of modern warfare. Just as the narrator begins to feel that he has misjudged the military profession, he encounters his new room-mate, Dee Jeter, and Jeter's renowned warrior father, Stud. Loyal to the corps, Stud and Dee are a gritty father-son combination that the narrator regards as the antithesis of Paul Marriott and *his* son, a college student. In fact, the narrator is close to attaching himself to Marriott as to a surrogate father. But Stud Jeter's death brings forth from Marriott his deepest feelings about life, and those feelings are about war and the courageous men who wage it rather than about Flaubert and fine wine. Paul Marriott's taste for literature and music, delightful and remarkable as it is, is a mere overlay to a strongly martial personality. As the story ends, the narrator realizes that the Marine Corps is truly a "mysterious community of men" from which he will always be excluded.

Styron returns time and again to the military service as a subject for his works. So prolonged was his experience with the marines, so deep its impression on him, that he cannot shake loose from its tenacious hold. With a mixture of nostalgia, loath-ing, fascination, and respect, Styron broods on the Marine Corps and tries to wrest from this unique institution a few of its secrets. He also reflects on warfare in general, and on the decline in idealistic principles in the wars since World War II. In all of Styron's writings on the subject—his novella, play, novel-in-progress, and essays—there is resistance to the esprit de corps of military service. The combat maneuvers and "salty locutions" bind the men into one unit at the price of their individuality and freedom. The bureaucratic war machine grinds up the unique personalities of those who serve it and spits out a gray mass of faceless ciphers. One result is that men may deny their human right and duty to make choices and to take responsibility for those choices. An essay on Lieutenant Calley and the war in Vietnam discusses and dismisses the cog-in-machine excuse for the commission of war crimes. In "Calley" and again in "Arnheiter," an analysis of a navy lieutenant's relief from command, Styron warns against "the potential for disaster that exists for us when at any level of authority there is a crucial abdication of personal responsibility." As we have seen, Al Mannix takes on the long march as a challenge to his integrity; Schwartz steals a book from the clap shack's doctor because he thinks it is the right thing to do. Rebellion against the powers-that-be is applauded on its own terms, as an assertion of the individual over the collective will, and it takes on added meaning when the officer class, epitomized by Calley in real life, Budwinkle in fiction, is an inferior species.

Waging war is a barbarous endeavor that somehow attracts as it repels. Styron joined the marines at age seventeen as much to prove his manliness as to fight the aggressor Japan. After all these years of disillusionment with the military he still sees that warfare may not only fail to extinguish the spark of nobility in men but may in fact fan that spark to a blaze. Part of his endless fascination with the Marine Corps and its unique brand of sadistic training is the realization that the boot-camp experience was a crucible that tested the mettle of each participant, willing or unwilling. Those who endured felt themselves changed for the better. So, too, war itself, in whatever form, puts human decency and courage on the line.

In Styron's view, World War II was the last just war in American eyes. The succeeding wars in Korea and Vietnam were entered into because of a fear of Communism. Styron distinguishes fear from hatred: it is right to hate Communism for its oppression and exploitation of the individual, but fear of the Communist menace leads the United States into countries and skirmishes where it does not belong. Such fear also drives someone like Lieutenant Calley toward the destruction of civilian women, children, and old men at Mai Lai. Calley has denied the code of honor among warriors that must remain operative if they are to remain human. As Styron puts it,

Few of us may be enamored of the military, but the military is both a fact of life and an institution; and like any institution—like law or business or government itself—it must stand guard against the venal, the felonious and the corrupt. Thus to ignore the lesson of Lieutenant Calley is to ignore a crucial reality: that war is still steadfastly a part of the human condition, and that our very survival as human beings continues to depend on accommodating ourselves to ancient rules of conduct.[6]

6

Speaking the Unspeakable:
Sophie's Choice

The most compelling theme in history—including the history of our own time—[is] that of the catastrophic propensity on the part of human beings to attempt to dominate one another.

—*New York Review of Books* , June 29, 1978

A central event in the twentieth century—indeed, in all of human history—is the Nazi extermination of millions of people in the concentration camps of Europe. Mostly Jews but also Gypsies, homosexuals, Poles, Greeks, and others assessed to be of impure blood were rounded up from their homes and herded into boxcars for mass shipment to slave-labor camps and eventual death by rifle fire, asphyxiation, or other modes of extinction. The occurrence, not to mention the meaning, of this event is so overwhelming that many who were not directly involved are afraid to approach it, awed into silence by the presumption and the pretension of understanding. But the subject matter is one that William Styron was almost destined to confront. In a sense he had been in training to confront it from the beginning of his literary career, for his foremost interest has been in the limits to human freedom that are placed by one person—or people—on another, which very often actually culminate in death. In *Sophie's Choice*, Styron explores the Holocaust through a fictional character with firsthand experience of it, who tells her story to a budding writer very much resembling Styron himself.

Styron approaches Sophie obliquely, through the use of a first-person narrator named Stingo. Many factors dictated this narrative technique. First, a sense of distance from the tragic events is needed to put them into perspective, to hold the horrors at arm's length, as it were, in order to study them and perhaps in order to cope with them. The reader, in fact, is twice removed, since the book is narrated by the mature Stingo looking backward. This mature writer, unlike his youthful self, has read the philosophical treatises and the firsthand memoirs about Nazi Germany and therefore sets the emotional events of his past into an intellectual context. Second, the frankly autobiographical nature of the narrator lends a certain authority to the story. Third, the narrator's comical or mundane experiences relieve what would otherwise be the unrelenting grimness of the central event, and simultaneously function as a foil to that event, setting off its monstrous proportions.

In actuality, there are three separate but related foci in *Sophie's Choice*: the concentration-camp experience, which prompts reflection on the meaning of evil; the artistic development of a fiction writer; and the sexual maturation of a post-pubescent young man. The first focus is of course the weightiest and most important in cultural terms; but equally important for the novel are the changes in Stingo's life during the summer of 1947. This is Stingo's story as much as it is Sophie's—perhaps even more. Styron, after all, does not pretend to understand Auschwitz.

The novel begins with an introduction to this young man called Stingo, his silly nickname—a derivative of Stinky—as good a commentary as any on his immaturity. Stingo is a stranger in a strange land, a rural Southerner in the northern metropolis of New York, and a would-be novelist forced to earn his living by passing judgment on other writers' literary endeavors. After quitting his unsatisfactory job in publishing, Stingo moves to cheaper quarters in Brooklyn and becomes a gentile in the kingdom of the Jews. Meeting Sophie and her boyfriend Nathan, co-boarders in Yetta Zimmerman's Flatbush Pink Palace, fills Stingo's solitary life with companions as well as the possibility of introductions to nubile and willing young ladies. An unexpected sum of money from Stingo's father back in Virginia supports the daily work on a first novel. Life holds forth its rich promise, beckoning the hero with visions of unlimited treasures.

As the mature Stingo writes, with an ironic though affectionate glance at his youthful self,

It was wonderful to be twenty-two and a little drunk, knowing that all went well at the writing desk, shiveringly happy in the clutch of one's own creative ardor and . . . the certitude that the wellsprings of youth would never run dry, and that wrenching anguish endured in the crucible of art would find its recompense in everlasting fame, and glory, and the love of beautiful women.[1]

For much of his recounting of Stingo's story, Styron uses an inflated rhetoric similar to the above. The prose is swollen and turgid, as tumescent as the young man's libido, bursting with energy and seeking release. The use of richly complex language is typical of Styron, who has often been accused of, and criticized for, overwriting.[2] In fact, Styron's ear for language allows him to vary the cadences in Sophie's Choice, so that the prose in the sections about the concentration camps seems matter-of-fact and pared down, even gray, whereas the prose in the sections about Stingo is multihued, almost lurid. This variation in style, a kind of double rhythm, again sets the two orders of experience against each other. And the arcane vocabulary and complex syntax of the Stingo sections define the character of the narrator's youthful incarnation: his passionate yearning to be a writer, coupled with his desire to write like the greats of the past whom he had encountered in his college English courses.

In Sophie's Choice, Styron has perfectly matched style to substance, continually veering back and forth between inflation and deflation in a way that not only elevates and undercuts the main character but also suits this character's alternating moods of elevation and despair. "Call me Stingo," the narrator's enjoinder to the reader, lends an element of grandeur to the story by implicitly inviting comparison to the opening of Moby-Dick. But it also quietly mocks the heroic aspirations of the narrator, whose name, unlike Ishmael's, is not one that any grown-up person would feel comfortable in uttering. Many of Styron's lengthy sentences also rhetorically contain in miniature the double rhythm of the novel as a whole. They begin by loftily describing an ideal and end by ruefully noting the reality. One good example concerns Stingo's first lodgings in New York:

I had been lured to this place . . . not alone by its name—which conjured up an image of Ivy League camaraderie, baize-covered lounge tables littered with copies of the *New Republic* and *Partisan Review,* and elderly retainers in frock coats fretting over messages and catering to one's needs—but by its modest rates: ten dollars a week. (p. 10)

The varied cadences of this sentence—the long, almost parenthetical phrase between the dashes, the abrupt phrase following the colon—recreate the humor of the situation and underscore several sets of double points of view, including literature versus commerce and illusion versus reality. Another double rhythm is found in the descriptions of the literature that Stingo must read for a living as opposed to the literature that he reads for pleasure after work hours and strains to emulate. *The Plumber's Wench* and *Harold Haarfagen, a Saga* do not measure up to Stingo's high standards, and his indignation or guilt at their low quality fills his reports with black humor, a juxtaposition of trash with treasure (although, ironically, the treasure of Stingo's youthful prose remains to be seen, and his taste is not totally trustworthy).

Fittingly, given the significance of Jews and Judaism to this novel, the style is reminiscent of the Jewish humor in the novels at the fore during the decade that Styron was writing this work (such as Joseph Heller's *Good as Gold*) and poised for their meteoric rise during the very year in which the novel is set.[3] The double rhythm of aspiration versus reality, contained in a style that continually pulls the rug out from under itself, is found as well in the sections of *Sophie's Choice* having to do with Stingo's feverish attempts to rid himself of his burdensome virginity. On the beach with the provocative Leslie Lapidus, Stingo's attention is "drawn over and over again to those astounding breasts, then to the navel, perfect little goblet from which, in a microsecond's fantasy, I lapped lemon Kool-Aid or some such nectar with my tongue." Only a misplaced country boy would fantasize Kool-Aid in that sophisticated navel. But not even Kool-Aid is to be lapped from Leslie Lapidus, who, though she rhymes with "Ah, feed us," cannot give Stingo the sexual nourishment he craves. A young man with big goals and limited attainments, Stingo and his dilemmas are mirrored in the style of the novel.

As already mentioned, the prose of the Stingo sections contrasts with the prose of the Sophie sections. In addition, Styron cleverly varies the style *within* the accounts by Sophie of her experiences during World War II: here, too, he sets up a double rhythm. Sophie and several other prisoners sleep in the basement of the house occupied by the commandant of Auschwitz, Rudolf Höss. (They are the equivalent, in the world of the twentieth-century European concentration camp, to the "house niggers" of nineteenth-century-American slavery.) The basement is described in matter-of-fact terms expressed monosyllabically: it is "damp and ill-lit and [stinks] of rot and mold." In contrast to the basement where Sophie resides is the attic where she works as Höss's secretary and translator: as she ascends the stairs she thinks how "Höss in his eyrie waited beneath the image of his Lord and Savior, waited in the celibate retreat of a calcimine purity so immaculate that even as Sophie approached, unsteadily, the very walls, it seemed, in the resplendent morning were washed by a blindingly incandescent, almost sacramental light." Styron's description of this attic office uses a complex syntax and polysyllabic vocabulary charged with religious fervor. For Höss's office is indeed a heavenly sanctuary to Sophie, a place where she cannot only play at normal pursuits but can also seize the opportunity to plead for her son's life. Her aspirations and expectations are shattered by Höss's failure to save her son through removal to the Lebensborn program; Sophie never sees Jan again, even though Höss had promised her a final meeting in his office. Her existence in the foul-smelling cellar is the true order of her life. The "higher" orders are morally degraded, a masquerade of normalcy, and an illusive safe harbor. The use of religious imagery to describe Höss's attic retreat is a satanic inversion befitting the hellish activities celebrated at the black mass of Auschwitz. A similar vocabulary of salvation dedicated to the machinery of death is found embroidered in the sampler in Emmi Höss's room: "Just as the Heavenly Father saved people from sin and from hell, Hitler saves the German Volk from destruction."

The two orders of experience described in the concentration camp simultaneously have little and everything to do with one another. The commandant and his children live in a tidy house with all the trappings of the good life and the freedom to enjoy them (though they must keep the windows closed to exclude the smell of burning flesh). The prisoners at the camp are nothings, reduced to the numbers tattooed on their wrists, subject to starvation, degradation, and, ultimately, extermination. Although there is no meaningful interaction between these orders they are dependent upon each other for their status and significance. Without Auschwitz, Höss is just another petty bureaucrat. Without Höss and the Nazis, Sophie and the others would be free. Seen together, these two orders of existence endlessly circle each other in a highly patterned but macabre dance of death.

The full horror of living death in the concentration camp cannot be easily comprehended. By setting up the rhythm of Stingo's life, Styron highlights by contrast the horrors of Sophie's nightmarish existence. While she is debarking from the crowded railway car at Auschwitz, about to make a horrible choice, Stingo is gorging himself on bananas in order to meet the minimum-weight requirements for induction into the marines. While she is hiding from the Nazis, in the Warsaw occupation, he is listening to Glenn Miller, swilling beer, and indulging in numerous other idle pleasures. Styron muses on the discrepancy and simultaneity of these two sets of events and the double order of existence that they reveal. Quoting philosopher George Steiner, from a book of essays entitled *Language and Silence* (1967), he puzzles over time: "Are there, as science fiction and Gnostic speculation imply, different species of time in the same world, 'good time' and enveloping folds of inhuman time, in which men fall into the slow hands of the living damnation?" Steiner's "notion of different orders of time simultaneous but in no effective analogy or communication" seems the only explanation for the failure of Stingo and others like him to sense the utter depravity even half a world away—to smell, as it were, the quantities of burning flesh. By creating Sophie to tell her story to

Stingo, Styron finds the nexus between the two orders of existence and the means to speak the unspeakable.

Sophie's dark tale is told in bits and pieces throughout the novel, a narrative technique that builds suspense. But this is more than just narrative technique—it is also a psychological case study of a woman in the throes of guilt, who can only very slowly reveal the horrible acts that she has herself committed. Sophie's narration of her past proceeds in fits and starts, with hitches caused by her significant omissions or actual lies. The rosy picture that she paints of life with her father in Cracow may be compared to her own face with her false teeth firmly in place: a vision of health, a charade, and an illusion. The reality of that life, and that father, is as frighteningly different as Sophie's caved-in face without her dentures, which Stingo inadvertently glimpses. Instead of being a man who saves Jews, Sophie's father is a Jew-hater who produces a pamphlet urging their extermination. Instead of loving her father, and working willingly as his secretary, Sophie detests the man but lacks the courage to refuse his orders. Faced with the task of first typing and then disseminating his rabid pamphlet, Sophie is unable to opt out of the job; she can only manage the small choice of refusing to accept her father's offer of tea. Indeed, she keeps a copy of the pamphlet hidden in her shoe at Auschwitz, and, pretending to be a Jew-hater herself, attempts to use it and her relationship with the man who created it as bargaining chips with Höss for preferential treatment. The complicity that she feels in her father's anti-Semitic endeavors causes Sophie the greatest difficulty in revealing the truth to Stingo as she recounts her past, and it prevents her from uttering a word of it to Nathan, the Jew. This complicity feeds her fear at being called Irma Griese—beautiful blonde killer of Jews at Auschwitz—during Nathan's drug-crazed orgies of hatred, since she recognizes a grain of truth in his accusations. Because of this recognition, the more he torments her the more she accepts it and even loves it, craving punishment for what she sees as her many evil choices.

Sophie's choices, as gradually revealed to Stingo, have been made by and large out of passivity and fear. She has bowed to the will of her father and her husband in the propagation of anti-

Semitism. She has refused to join her friend Wanda and lover
Joseph in the Resistance movement. True, she does steal a ham
for her tubercular mother and attempts to steal a radio for the
Auschwitz prisoners, but both daring maneuvers have been cir-
cumvented, feeding her sense of worthlessness. Sophie's ultimate choice, the one to be made between her two children, is so
horrific that she cannot reveal it until the end: the end of her life
and hence the end of the novel. Only gradually, in fact, does she
reveal the very existence of these children, much less her complicity in the execution of Eva at Birkenau. A victim of outside
forces, with no inner resources with which to seize control of her
life, Sophie finds that her passivity has shaped her destiny and
brought her to the threshold of this terrible choice, sneeringly
called a privilege by the doctor who forces her to make it. Who
shall live and who shall die?—a choice that recapitulates the
choices made every day by the Nazis at Auschwitz, and puts her
in their camp morally as well as physically.

Sophie's greatest urge, that toward life, has caused her to
place her children's welfare above all other priorities. Thus, her
choice at the threshold of Auschwitz is an especially cruel burden. And its blackness only deepens, for she cannot save even
the child she has picked to live. (Presumably Jan dies later, his
temporary lease on life only an unfulfillable dream to torment
his mother.) Sophie herself lives on in a death-in-life existence
that mocks the very notion of life. After Auschwitz, only a delib-
erate suppression of the past enables Sophie to carry on. Her
attachment to Nathan Landau is inevitable, given her guilt and
self-loathing, as is her relationship with Stingo: the one her
executioner, the other her father-confessor.

Paradoxically, Nathan Landau is Sophie's savior as well as
her executioner, so firmly intertwined in the novel, as in Styron's
world view, are love and death. While in the concentration
camp, Sophie had struggled to stay alive at any cost. Her passive
acquiescence to the lesbian advances of the housekeeper Wilhe-
mine and her active sexual pursuit of Rudolf Höss were nothing
more than attempts to make it through one more day in order to
steal a radio, to save her child's life, or to snatch a few more
moments from the jaws of death. "Liberation" from Auschwitz

eventually places on her shoulders the terrible burden of freedom, setting her forth into a life requiring constant choice-making, alone and with an eternity of grief before her. It is *after* liberation that Sophie makes her suicide attempt, and even at this act she fails. Her death-in-life continues in her new home in America, until Nathan arrives like an avenging angel to save her from the browbeating of the bureaucrat in the Brooklyn College Library, as well as from the pernicious physical aftereffects of her concentration-camp existence. It is Nathan who makes Sophie "to bloom like a rose," with his massive infusion of iron and his massive doses of love.

At Auschwitz, the omnipresence of death had stifled Sophie's sexual urges. Now, having been liberated by Nathan not only from the physical subjection of her Nazi oppressors but also from the sexual repressiveness of her Catholic upbringing, Sophie comes into the full flower of her womanhood. Her love-making with Nathan is vigorous and larger than life. Stingo, an unwilling eavesdropper from his downstairs apartment, describes it as "no mere copulatory rite but a tournament, a rumpus, a free-for-all, a Rose Bowl, a jamboree." But these episodes of intense and joyful intimacy are continually followed by violent arguments that often culminate in physical abuse. The force of Nathan's emotions invariably drives the lovers apart and just as invariably propels them back together. The double rhythm of the novel manifests itself in these alternating experiences of desire and despair, intimacy and isolation, rage and peace, life and death.

Nathan himself embodies as a character the doubleness of the novel that is expressed so well through plot, theme, and style. A self-professed scientist, Nathan Landau is in search of the cure for humankind's most dread diseases. Sophie, in fact, mistakes him for a physician when they first meet, led astray by his knowledge of illnesses and their cures. He has moods of intense calm in which he sits quietly with Sophie, reciting Emily Dickinson or listening to Beethoven's Fourth Symphony. He has upsurges of joy during which he tells screamingly funny jokes and cannot sit still, so rampaging is the life force in his veins. But there are other sides to Nathan's personality, fueled by the fury and venom, rage and disorder, that are bottled up inside. In his black moods he toasts death instead of life and extols suicide. At home in the two cultures of science and humanities, Nathan Landau is woefully unfit for the world at large. Naziism, which he analogizes to cancer, utterly possesses him. His obsession with the Holocaust accounts in part for his attraction to Sophie, who has firsthand knowledge of it; but it also causes him to detest Sophie for her Polish, non-Jewish origins, and to berate her for living when others have died. Nathan's fury is undoubtedly largely self-directed, since he is himself a Jew of military age who did not fight—much less die—for his people. So full of life, Nathan is paradoxically a death wish waiting for fulfillment. In Connecticut, Nathan beats, kicks, and degrades Sophie and swears her to a suicide pact. Sophie absorbs his verbal and physical abuse, collecting it into "some cellar or dustbin within her being where she has stored up all his savagery." This cellar or dustbin is reminiscent of her basement quarters in Höss's home, symbol of her degradation at the hands of the Nazis. A victim of Höss and his regime, Sophie is no less a victim of her savior, Nathan Landau.

Nathan's brother eventually reveals to Stingo the horrible key to Nathan's alternating moods: not only is Nathan a drug addict, he is also a certified paranoid schizophrenic. His personal history is a sham, for he has never been to college, much less to Harvard, as he claimed. His life's work is a charade, for he is not a biologist on the verge of a scientific breakthrough. Just as Sophie knows nothing of Nathan's lies or omissions, so he knows little of hers. She doesn't tell him of her father's anti-Semitic propaganda, and although Sophie discloses the fact that she has had one child, she conceals the existence of the other as well as Eva's manner of death. The two lovers enact an elaborate masquerade and go to their deaths without revealing their deepest secrets to each other.

The costumes that Sophie and Nathan wear on their death beds symbolize the masquerade of their lives together. But if these outlandish costumes are lies, they serve the purpose of masking despair and giving Sophie and Nathan a momentary hold on life. The full meaning of Sophie's range of costumes—

period pieces from pre-Holocaust eras, the thirties back to the Gay Nineties and even earlier—cannot be fathomed unless her existence in the concentration camp is recalled. There, Sophie is stripped of her clothes and allowed to wear only a drab cotton smock like everyone else. Divested of her individuality, Sophie is turned into a nonbeing, a number tattooed on her wrist; she finds that she cannot remember her name, or who she is. When she is released from the camp and arrives in the United States, she is especially vulnerable to assaults from the faceless mob, and Styron expresses her reaction to one such event, a groping hand on the subway, in terms of nakedness and clothing: "She who had for so long been on and off literally naked and who, these few months in Brooklyn, had so painstakingly reclothed herself in self-assurance and sanity had again by this act . . . been stripped bare. And she felt once more the freezing cold of the spirit." It is no wonder that Sophie likes to dress up with Nathan—to clothe herself not only in self-assurance and sanity but also in cheerfulness and joy. It may be that Nathan has been similarly deprived of his individuality by incarceration in a variety of mental institutions. Certainly he takes to this costuming with great exuberance, instructed about clothing by Sophie herself. Sophie had been deprived not only of her clothing but also of the body on which her clothing rested. Even Nathan's miraculous diagnosis and continual ministrations cannot restore her missing teeth or firm her slack flesh. So as she begins to bloom into health she begins to show off her body, almost defiantly, since the costumes draw great attention to her. The most gala of occasions—when Nathan will make his great pronouncement of his scientific breakthrough—brings forth Sophie's most daring outfit, with decolletage that is unusual for her. Nathan also transforms himself for the occasion with a fancy white linen suit. The two promenade forth dressed to the nines, veritable peacocks in a drab and colorless world.

It is not surprising that Stingo is enormously attracted to the couple. Stingo has in his own small way flouted a bureaucracy, by refusing to wear a hat at McGraw-Hill publishing where hats are the uniform of the day. He has felt, but never heard anyone enunciate, that self-expression through dress is a basic human right, even a duty, and that in its highest form it approaches art. The touch of eccentricity and exhibitionism in Nathan and Sophie's costumery seems a good thing to the young, rebellious Stingo in search of his own identity. The costumes and the daring they represent seduce Stingo into a relationship with the couple, in spite of the violent and self-destructive behavior that had previously frightened him away. It is as if he hopes some of their glamour, excitement, and style will rub off on him. And, of course, he is lonely.

Another tie that early binds Stingo to the two lovers is their common passion for music. Nathan can afford a phonograph and records, and music is always sifting down to Stingo from the apartment above. No longer does Stingo have to spend hours in the record stores; through Nathan and Sophie he has access to the "divine breath" of classical music. Nathan's offer of these records when he and Sophie are at work seems incredibly generous to Stingo, since records in the 1940s are costly and breakable. Because of Nathan, Stingo is never deprived of "this or that wrenching harmony, or some miraculously stitched tapestry of the baroque." Indeed, music fills the pages of *Sophie's Choice* as it fills Stingo's life. It serves as part of the construction of the novel as well as background to the plot. One interviewer has remarked to Styron that the book struck him "as a conscious *alteration* of the somber and the humorous: along the lines of some large musical form—a suite , . . or a symphony. . . . not only slow and fast movements, but . . . *scherzos* alternating with *marches funebres, bourees* with *graves*. . . . " Styron has agreed that a musical sensibility is helpful for understanding a novel in which one of the major points of sensibility is music.[4]

A love of music is a passion that Sophie and Nathan share, which feeds their passion for one another. One of Sophie's first purchases in the United States is an inexpensive radio that she keeps by her bedside in order to fill her nights with the music of which the concentration camp had deprived her. Music alone fills her with serenity and hope that her life might now be different. After her degrading experience on the New York subway, her spirit is buoyed only by the "mysteriously therapeutic powers of W. A. Mozart, M.D."; and after her collapse in the Brook-

lyn College Library, when she is carried home by Nathan, she
applies to herself the medicine she craves: a dose of Beethoven's
Pastoral Symphony. Sophie had once wished to be a teacher of
music. Now, music is for her not only a source of joy but also a
nostalgic look backward to what might have been but never was,
at least for her. Like the flamboyant costumery that she wears to
assert her individuality, classical music represents a world franti-
cally clutched but eternally elusive. The music that she loves
conjures a Europe in halcyon days, "a Europe of almost inconceivable sweetness"—a Europe of Sophie's wildest imaginings,
which she could never have experienced.

It almost seems to the reader of *Sophie's Choice* that musical
notes emanate from the pages of the book. In the scenes of
the novel set in Yetta's boarding house, Sophie's phonograph
continually pours forth Bach, Haydn, Beethoven, Mozart, or
Brahms. Because she plays the phonograph loudly, and because
the windows are kept open to catch the slightest summer breeze,
the music reverberates throughout the house and into the street.
It sets a tone or provides counterpoint to the action. After Sophie
and Nathan's lusty copulatory rites, the slow movement of Beethoven's Fourth Symphony incongruously begins. Following
Nathan's orgy of rage at Sophie, which leads to their moving
from Yetta's, Haydn plays on in Sophie's empty room, his sweet,
symmetrical cadences contributing to Stingo's feeling of irre-
trievable loss. Sophie and Nathan listen to classical music
throughout the afternoon of their suicide, including Mozart's
larghetto from the B-flat-major piano concerto, the last he wrote,
whose tragic measures had once seemed to Sophie to contain "a
resignation that was almost like joy." The record on the top of the
stack, which Stingo supposes is the last they heard, is Bach's
Jesu, Joy of Man's Desiring. For Stingo, thinking of these two lost
souls estranged from God, the music is especially poignant.

Whenever the characters move out of the womblike existence at Yetta's house, strains of music follow them. Nathan sings
Don Giovanni along with the radio in his car as he and Sophie
speed off to a party at Marty Haber's; an opera about a descent
into hell and the return of a father ghost is wholly appropriate to
the novel. But much of the music that plays outside of Sophie

and Nathan's control is music of a different sort. The Andrews Sisters croon "Don't Fence Me In" over the jukebox, in the restaurant to which the main characters adjourn to celebrate Nathan's self-proclaimed scientific breakthrough. Later, in the same restaurant, when Sophie confides in Stingo about Rudolf Höss, the same popular tune provides a commentary on her tale. As the concentration camp deprived Sophie of her freedom, so her relationship with Nathan, in some ways so liberating, has utterly circumscribed her life, to the extent that the only release lies in death.

Popular music resounds as well in the sections concerning Sophie's life at Auschwitz. Prisoners stepping down from the boxcars are greeted by a bizarre live band of prisoner-musicians in an off-key rendition of "La Cumparsita." Eva and her enchanted flute—both a small piping in the cacophony at Auschwitz—are snatched away from Sophie, to be replaced by Emmi and her radio, playing "dreamy, modern ersatz-Strauss waltzes" and other "soft murmurous schmaltz." When Sophie takes her last leave of Rudolf Höss, hoping against hope that he will save her son Jan, she passes by Emmi's room and decides not to steal the radio after all. As if in mockery of her choice, the radio plays the overture to an operetta by Franz Lehár, the Commandant's favorite composer; the name of the operetta is *The Land of Smiles*. In addition, the phonograph in the parlor plays constantly, and strains of "noisy German backyard schmaltz" reach Sophie in the attic office where she attempts to seduce Höss. One favorite record, "The Beer Barrel Polka," gets stuck in a groove, and endlessly repeats the mocking word *fun*, in "we'll have a barrel of fun-fun-fun." The total effect of these musical pieces, all singularly out of tune with the grim business being conducted, is to enhance the double rhythm of the novel as a whole. Yet it cannot be assumed that Styron is using classical music as a moral touchstone, to separate the good characters from the bad. Although Sophie in her loathing for her father thinks of him as "everything that music cannot be"—presumably crude, insensitive, and, above all, detestable—in fact two equally despicable, rabidly anti-Semitic characters have the same musical sensibilities and high culture as Sophie: Walter Dürrfeld, the German industrialist, whose talents help to build Auschwitz; and the Polish Princess Czartoryska, who wants to establish a fund for driving the Jews out of her country. That their musical taste is so out of rhythm with their moral sense is particularly mysterious and unnerving to Sophie and presumably to Styron.

As already stated, Sophie forges her bond with Nathan partly on the basis of a shared love for music. A life without Nathan is for her as inconceivable as a life without Beethoven. When she flees Brooklyn with Stingo, after Nathan threatens their lives, the barrenness of her prospects is symbolized by the Muzak that insinuates itself into her consciousness on the train to Richmond. Surely one of the factors that propels her northward again, away from Stingo and the life he offers, is the fact that the radio stations in the South play no classical music other than what is broadcast from the Metropolitan Opera on a Saturday afternoon. Music is not only in Sophie's blood, it *is* her life's blood. Without it she will die.

Of course, even *with* music Sophie will die—and she does die, in part, because her burden of guilt is too heavy to carry any longer. This overwhelming guilt and self-loathing have strengthened her attachment to Nathan Landau, and to his death urge. Moreover, a pattern of dependency on a dominating father figure was set early in childhood, so that what Nathan now commands, Sophie will accomplish. "I think you have absolutely no ego at all," Nathan says to her fondly, after she spends hours and travels miles to find a certain pastry he has idly mentioned. Sophie knows that this lack of ego, or strong sense of self, has propelled her into many humiliating situations, including lying prone beneath Nathan as he tries to urinate in her mouth. One may even go one step further, wondering if her utter quiescence of will is related to her femaleness, and whether it has led to her earmarking her daughter for extinction rather than her son. Ultimately, Sophie's loss of faith in God contributes to her feelings of hopelessness and helplessness, and to her dependency on Nathan, without whom she feels she is nothing. Unwilling to be left behind once again, she enters into a death pact with her lover.

Styron has defined absolute evil as "total domination of human beings by others up to the point of extermination."[5] Seen in this light, Nathan Landau's hold over Sophie would be absolutely evil except for the fact that he is certifiably insane. In contrast, the Nazis were calculating and controlled; they exemplify what Styron, following Hannah Arendt, discusses as the "banality of evil." Instead of devils in black capes, Auschwitz and the other camps contained petty bureaucrats pushing pencils. This is the real horror of the Holocaust, not that God was absent but that humanity was absent. To Styron, Sophie's conception of God as a monster, an idea that causes her to recoil from the nuns in the restaurant, is totally beside the point. He even surmises that it is a search for God that propels the Nazi officer at the train station into giving Sophie a "choice;" estranged from God, and yearning for Him, the officer needs to feel a sense of sin in order to reach the opposite state, grace. Therefore he bullies Sophie into this horrible decision.

Following her confrontation with evil, it is apparent why Sophie does not fit in with the college graduates who gather on Coney Island. Their palavering about Freud and sex—fashionable topics in the late 1940s—and worrying over oedipal dependencies and transference problems fill her with disgust, not because of her stern Catholic upbringing, but rather because their discussion amounts only to picking at little scabs. As Sophie puts it, these indulged Americans have "unearned unhappiness." Styron scatters many scenes about Freud and sex throughout *Sophie's Choice*, with several purposes in mind. First, he uses them to paint a picture of an era in our history, in which attitudes toward sex were in painful flux. Second, he contrasts the orally expressive but physically repressive nature of modern American lovemaking with the total sexual experimentation and joy of Sophie's liberated practices. Third, he sets off the grimness of Sophie's own earned unhappiness, and provides some comic relief in the process. And fourth, he characterizes the narrator, Stingo, who is single-mindedly occupied with the attempt to lose his virginity.

When, inevitably, Stingo does lose his virginity it is just as inevitably with Sophie herself. Ironically, given the tie between religion and sexual repression, it is in his masquerade as the

Reverend Entwhistle (a ploy for checking into a Washington hotel room during the trip South from New York to Richmond) that Stingo succeeds in bedding the object of his desire. His sexual fulfillment follows Sophie's complete admission of her role in Eva's death, and her unbounded eroticism is more than an expression of simple joy in life; it is a "flight from memory and grief" and an "attempt to beat back death." With dawn, of course, comes Sophie's inevitable guilt at betraying her lover, forcing her back to Nathan.

Stingo had fantasized about his marriage bed with Sophie, wondering whether it would be large enough to accommodate their lovemaking. At the end he stands over Sophie's real marriage bed, the one in Yetta's boarding house on which she and Nathan now lie intertwined in death. His recognition of this inevitable linking of love and death, the womb-and-tomb nature of Sophie and Nathan's relationship, leads him to read over their common grave the poem by Emily Dickinson beginning "Ample make this bed." Sophie and Nathan find perfect unity and peace only through death. It remains for Stingo the writer to bear witness to their suffering, and in the telling of their tale to offer evidence of life and hope.

The saga of Sophie Zawistowska and Nathan Landau is one that Stingo could write only after years of reflection. The novel that he produces is a novel of becoming, charting the narrator's crossing the threshold from late adolescence into manhood, from a person who writes to a writer. After his stint in the military, Stingo thought he would never hear a shot again, nor would he be privy to violence and strife. Writing his novel about Maria Hunt, the beautiful suicide, had kept emotional upheaval at bay, served as an outlet for fear and dread, and distanced him from life. By becoming drawn to Sophie, Stingo is pulled into her life lived at the extreme. The summer of 1947 marks the time when Stingo became acquainted—truly acquainted, all his senses engaged—with love and death. Many of his actual subjects were already imagined by him: Stingo catalogues the novels he will write, including all the ones that Styron actually did write between *Lie Down in Darkness* (originally called *Inheritance of Night*) and *Sophie's Choice*, leaving out only *Set This House on Fire* because Stingo/Styron has not yet gone to Italy. But the vision of life that will color and impel those novels is a vision crystallized in that fateful summer. It is a vision that is as double as everything else in *Sophie's Choice*, for it speaks of comedy as well as tragedy, of joy as well as pain.

Out of all the blackness, epitomized by Sophie's choice at the jaws of hell, there is one hope to be excavated: that love is possible in such a world. The hope is frail, but also, in Styron's word, perdurable. In the fall of the year Stingo returns to Coney Island and the empty Steeplechase Park, where echoes of joyful roller-coaster rides seem to resound through the silent air. Stingo has himself fallen from innocence into experience, expelled from the amusement park of his youth. By asserting the possibilities for human decency and love, Stingo defiantly asserts his innocence anew—but an earned innocence, which sees the light as well as the darkness, and trusts in the former as it recognizes the full extent of the latter. Stingo has his own guilts to shoulder, including living off an inheritance gained through the sale of a slave; forsaking his cancer-ridden mother because of the demands her invalidism made on him; and abdicating his responsibility to act fully on his knowledge of Nathan's dementia. There is much for which to weep and atone, but it is possible for Stingo, as it is not for Sophie, to come to terms with his imperfections and to go on. Falling asleep on the beach, Stingo dreams that he is being buried alive, but in the morning wakens to find that two children have protectively covered him with sand. Waking to face a new day, with new possibilities, is a small resurrection to be sure, but it is a resurrection nonetheless. Stingo/Styron eventually finds a way to resurrect Sophie as well, for the making of art is a religious act that offers its own kind of rebirth for the dead.

7

~~~~~~~~~~~~~~~~~~~~~~~~~~~~~~~~~~~~~~~

The Search for a
Meaningful Theme

*One of the crucial struggles that any writer of significance has
had to endure is his involvement in the search for a meaningful
theme.*

—*Harper's*, April 1968

"In my career as a writer," the mature Stingo notes in *Sophie's
Choice*, "I have always been attracted to morbid themes—suicide,
rape, murder, military life, marriage, slavery." In this respect
Stingo is clearly identifiable with his creator, William Styron,
whose tragic sense of life has dictated his choice of subject matters and marked his entire literary output. This is not to say that
Styron's works are without humor. To the contrary, a humorous
streak runs deep in Styron. Some of his earliest attempts at
artistic creations, collected and retained by his father, are copies
of funny-paper cartoons. And while at college at Davidson, he
wrote satires for *Scripts 'n Pranks*.[1] Many of the episodes in his
mature work are very funny indeed, like Cass Kinsolving's en-
counter with the nubile Jehovah's Witness, but the comedy is
usually of the satiric or "black humor" variety. Even the catalog
of morbid themes listed above contains a joke—the inclusion of
marriage amongst rape, murder, and slavery—although the joke
is deadly serious, as any reader of *Lie Down in Darkness* will
attest.

What causes a writer to have a certain temperament that he
expresses in his works may be as much a matter of genetics as of
upbringing, but the genetic factor is too shrouded in mystery to
invite speculation. The circumstances of Styron's early life, easier to analyze, no doubt contributed greatly to his belief that

human beings hover perpetually on the brink of disaster, and thus contributed to his selection of morbid themes. His mother was an invalid throughout his childhood, and her early death, when Styron was a young teenager, left him disoriented and guilt ridden. The father's remarriage not long after brought into the family constellation a stepmother so unacceptable to Styron that she takes on in his memory dimensions of the evil witch in a hundred fairy tales; it was not until after her death, a few years ago, that Styron made these feelings public and drew a connection between his stepmother and the character of Helen in *Lie Down in Darkness*.[2] Then, at the tender age of eighteen, Styron found himself in a war for which he was not prepared, his freedom gone, his life in danger. These early experiences seem to have instilled in him a feeling of helplessness and a sensitivity to the idea of evil. His southern heritage, so he believes, predisposed him toward a well-developed sense of mortality and a kinship with the "silent majority" of the dead.[3]

In his difficult formative years, Styron obtained a measure of stability from his father. He draws affectionate portraits of the man in *Set This House on Fire* and *Sophie's Choice*, as well as in "Marriott, the Marine." The failed father–son relationships in such other works as *Lie Down in Darkness* (Milton and his deceased father), *The Confessions of Nat Turner* (Nat and his master Sam), and, by implication, *The Long March* and *In the Clap Shack* (Culver and Colonel Templeton, Magruder and Captain Glanz) all receive their impetus from the important and positive relationship that Styron enjoyed with his own father. Indeed, the influence of William Clark Styron, Sr., on his son's literary career cannot be overestimated. His faith and pride in his only child were manifested in many ways, not the least of which was the financial support that enabled this recent college graduate to devote himself to his first novel. Just as importantly, the elder Styron's liberal attitude toward blacks freed his son from certain constraints of his southern heritage and steered him toward an interest in slavery that would result most dramatically and obviously in *The Confessions of Nat Turner*. It is a mark of Styron's having been brought up in his particular southern household, in a segregated society, that relations between the black and white

races figure so importantly in his works, and that he struggled
so valiantly to come to know the black man.

William Styron's Southernness is in fact central to an understanding of this author. The South, alone among regions of the
United States, has a tragic past and a well-developed historical
sense with which to contemplate it. Styron frequently turns his
attention to this past, particularly to slavery, and to the legacy of
guilt that the past imposes on the present. Stingo lives the life of
an artiste in Brooklyn thanks to the life of a Virginia slave named
Artiste, whose sale netted a profit for Stingo's ancestors and
hence a financial cushion for Stingo. Cass Kinsolving's bizarre,
self-punishing behavior in Europe is finally traceable to a racially
motivated episode from his past, in a backwater town in Virginia. No matter where Styron's characters flee, their southern
roots cling tenaciously and, in some cases, threaten to choke
them with guilt. The same may be said of Styron.

Having lived in the North for forty years, Styron does not
consider himself a southern writer but rather an American writer with southern roots. Indeed, the "South" has essentially dis-
appeared, a situation deplored grandiloquently by Alfred Leverett in *Set This House on Fire*. Nonetheless, Styron grew up
among many then-viable southern traditions that have influenced his art. Years of reading the King James version of the
Bible are evident in the cadences and orotundity of his prose,
and religion is an important force in his works. The notion of
storytelling as a good in itself has led to the frequent use of a
first-person narrator to pull the reader into a yarn, and Styron
always tells a good story, no matter what else he is also trying to
do. Since Southerners traditionally feel "connected up," Styron
places a great emphasis on family and community, and on good
manners as the glue in these relationships. A "knifeblade of
nostalgia for the rural South," as Stingo calls it, cuts through
Styron's fiction regardless of specific setting or subject.

Yet, for all these southern markers, Styron's fiction is not
what one thinks of when one thinks of southern literature. His
"landscape" is different. It is more than a matter of changes in
architecture, the California influence replacing antebellum man-
sions. All of Styron's characteristically southern attributes are

created with a distinctively modern, hence non-southern twist. Their Bible reading notwithstanding, his characters find that faith is notably absent from their lives. Humans as Styron pictures them are cut off and estranged from God, left to find their salvation in strictly human terms. The situation is one that might be termed "existentialist," with an emphasis on making one's way in the here and now, with no guidance from above. There are only two major figures in Styron's works whose spiritual thirst is slaked by religion: Ella Swan in *Lie Down in Darkness* and Poppy Kinsolving in *Set This House on Fire*. Although Styron admires these women and envies their faith, he clearly believes that their way is not his way, for they lack the tragic sense. Moreover, religion is a malignant force in many cases, affording justification for human abuse and degradation. Helen Loftis, for example, attends church regularly and adopts a holier-than-most-everyone attitude that enables her to go on spewing forth hate. The clerics of the South in *The Confessions of Nat Turner* use the Bible to account for and perpetuate the institution of slavery; and Nat himself relies on Old Testament prophesy supplemented by direct messages from God to incite blood letting and carnage. Only a contemplation of Margaret Whitehead herself brings Nat to a rapprochement with God, and the envisioned oneness is more sexual than spiritual. Finally, Dr. Jemand von Niemand quotes scripture and searches for God as he forces Sophie into her inhuman choice.

The traditional southern emphasis on family and community also comes under scrutiny in Styron's works. *The Confessions of Nat Turner* reveals how closely the very notion of family is bound up with the color of one's skin in the nineteenth-century South: the blacks do not enjoy the luxury of a sanctioned family or community life, and close relationships are subject at any time to dissolution according to the whim of the ruling caste. In the twentieth-century South, in the upper-middle class, the situation is reversed, if one may generalize from *Lie Down in Darkness*. The white families have lost their central core and are held together by only the weakest threads that break under the pressures of modern life. Family cohesiveness is still an important goal, to be sought at all costs, but it is not a given of one's birth. Helen Loftis struggles to maintain the appearance of a unified family but this family is all sham and no substance. No larger community supports and strengthens individual families in their times of need: the country club as a common meeting ground does not bind people together in any significant way. In contrast, the black families in *Lie Down in Darkness* share significantly in each other's lives and escape isolation through their involvement in the larger religious group. Ella Swan's kinships are real and sustaining, although by white standards hers is a "broken" family. Good manners as traditionally defined are singularly absent from Styron's depictions of the blacks: invitations are not tendered when they are not meant, sweetness is not expressed when anger is felt, what things look like is not as important as what they are.

The southern appreciation for gentility comes under attack by Styron in several instances, most directly in Albert Berger's remark to Peyton Loftis that southerners put manners before morals. By "manners" Styron implies large codes of behavior that include but are not limited to writing bread-and-butter notes and standing for your elders. Certainly, Milton Loftis maintains the illusion of propriety while carrying on an adulterous affair, and Helen Loftis behaves in a civilized way toward her husband's mistress while being destroyed from within by her implacable hatred. Too great a respect for manners accompanies Stingo to the North and results in a serious misjudgment of Nathan Landau, whom Stingo pegs as poorly behaved rather than as mentally ill. Predetermined patterns of interaction are woefully inadequate in dealing with the societies in dissolution that Styron depicts. When things fall apart because of the stresses of modern existence, including urbanization and technological "advances" (like the gas chambers and the atom bomb), good manners cannot hold them together. Styron believes in the necessity for respectful modes of behavior and sympathizes with Stingo's father for his outrage at the ill-mannered New York taxicab driver with whom he comes in conflict; but Styron also recognizes that manners are not absolute but rather defined by every culture, and that they are often wrongly accepted as ends in themselves rather than as a means toward civilized relationships.

Along with the other southern qualities that Styron calls

into question must be included even the place and worth of storytelling. Telling stories is indubitably a human rather than a solely southern activity, but Southerners are traditionally adept at it: the stereotype pictures two or more kin or neighbor folks rocking on the front porch, sipping lemonade, and swapping yarns. This rich oral tradition may have pointed Styron toward his favorite narrative technique, the "call me Stingo" trick, but at the same time, Styron does not find it to be an unqualified good. Time and again he shows the need for unraveling the lies that humans tell to escape the weight of the truth of their sordid existences. Mason Flagg regales Peter Leverett with stories about his daring escapades—military and sexual—during the last war, and his exciting work in the theater; Nathan Landau holds Stingo and Sophie spellbound with tantalizing tales of scientific breakthroughs; Sophie paints glowing pictures of her sainted father. Lying, which is a certain kind of storytelling, is endemic in society. At its worst it destroys trust and may do actual harm. Mason Flagg's "entertainments," for example, give form to his antisocial tendencies and allow them to grow unchecked.

At its best, storytelling weaves lifelines that enable people to survive trauma and tragedy: Sophie's life lasts only as long as her illusions and Michele Ricci is sustained by Cass's embellishments on America as the land of plenty. The art of storytelling as an ersatz form of psychoanalysis seems to have been William Styron's lifeline as well. "One sheds one's sicknesses in one's books," D. H. Lawrence said, a sentiment with which Styron would agree. In his rootless adolescent years, in battle with his stepmother and estranged from religion, Styron found more than relief—salvation is not too strong a word—in the creation of art, in the telling of *his* story under the guise of fiction, often with the immediacy and intimacy of first-person narration. Ever since, writing has lent stability to his life and given voice to his conflicts. Not a particularly glib speaker, bordering on the stumbling on occasion, Styron is singularly articulate on paper. His works testify to a world view that sees conflict and catastrophe at every turn.

Throughout his career, Styron has made clear his belief that human beings, not a higher force, are the agents of these disasters. The universe is "benign or indifferent" to human activity and God is probably nonexistent. Styron's fiction dwells, as he says in an interview, on

> human institutions: humanly contrived situations which cause people to live in wretched unhappiness. And this seems to be the largest mystery of human existence. Why we here on earth—we fellow human beings, theoretically a family—should find ourselves in such constant and universal discord: not supportive of each other, not sympathetic, not loving, but filled with hate and revenge and the desire to annihilate our own kind.[4]

From the smallest level of the nuclear family unit to the largest level of international relations, human beings are continually engaged in struggles for power and dominance. The Loftises in *Lie Down in Darkness* are unable to live in harmony: Milton and Peyton are allies in the war against Helen and Maude, and no one emerges the winner. Americans in search of a national identity in *Set This House on Fire* achieve a sense of self only by exploiting other cultures, epitomized by the attitude of Mason Flagg toward the Italians and by his treatment of Francesca Ricci and Cass Kinsolving. Meanwhile, Cass has forged his own cultural identity by dominating a group even weaker than he, the American black. Military service gives license to imperialistic and aggressive impulses, and its bureaucracies stifle individual thought and action: these are the morbid themes of *The Long March* and *In the Clap Shack*, and they will no doubt inform *The Way of the Warrior* as well.

In a 1960s article on the generation of the 1940s, Styron declared that his generation's "interminable experience with ruthless power and the loony fanaticism of the military mind" had caused it to be passionately antiwar. Indeed, the best of his generation, he argued, had grown more radical with age, empathizing with youth who struggled "with the managerial beast, military, secular, or scholastic."[5] Strongly individualistic himself, outrightly rebellious as a youth, Styron has always inveighed against bureaucracy and tyranny of any sort. His sympathies invariably lie with those he sees as victims of imprisoning human institutions: Peyton Loftis, ruined because of her family constellation; Cass Kinsolving, held in thrall to Mason Flagg and, by implication, to American materialism; Al Mannix, subject to the vagaries of the war machine; Wally Magruder, incarcerated by virtue of medical technology and the military hierarchy; Nat Turner and Sophie Zowistaska, enslaved by elaborate and rigorous caste systems. In his journalistic pieces as well, Styron often takes as his subject matter the abridgement of individual rights perpetrated by the American government on its citizens. One notorious case, that of a Connecticut killer named Benjamin Reid, elicited Styron's impassioned plea for the abolishment of capital punishment as well as for the improvement of our prisons and the entire penal system. Essays on this subject are collected in *This Quiet Dust*, in a section tellingly called "Victims," for he sees Reid as a Totally Damned American, unlucky enough to be born poor and black. Like fellow writers Norman Mailer and William Buckley, Styron got personally involved with a prisoner and met only betrayal, since his efforts on behalf of Reid were followed not by Reid's rehabilitation but by his commission of another crime. Yet Styron maintains his interest and belief in Benjamin Reid, for reasons he cannot totally comprehend. Agreeing with the appropriateness of a term that has been snidely applied to him, "jail groupie," Styron explains his attraction to such people as Reid on the basis of their exemplifying a metaphysical quality that we all share, the human condition of being victims.[6]

Styron's stand against capital punishment has intensified in the more than twenty years since his piece on Benjamin Reid. In November 1984 he participated in an event at Duke University called "Lone Vigil," reading selections from his works that highlight what he sees as society's false values and abridgement of human rights. At that time, Velma Barfield had recently been executed in North Carolina and Linwood Briley in Virginia (in terms of numbers, capital punishment is largely a southern phenomenon), and Styron argued that disturbed people should be segregated from society rather than put to death. No reason validates the death penalty, except vengeance, but "vengeance has no place in our system of justice." A "diehard abolitionist" of the death penalty, as he calls himself, Styron maintains that society must not use execution as an easy way out of confronting good and evil.[7] He hedges on this subject when asked whether a Nazi like Rudolf Höss deserves capital punishment, even answering:

Oh yes. No question about it. . . . There's absolutely no question that you can make exceptions about capital punishment. I make them all the time. Yet even for the most loathsome, atrocious civil crimes there is absolutely no justification, in my mind, for capital punishment. But on the level of the Nazi phenomenon, I don't think we can talk about capital punishment in the same way. It would have been a delicious pleasure to have seen Höss and Hitler and all that gang hanged: without qualification.[8]

Perhaps Styron, like Nathan Landau, analogizes Nazism to a cancer that must be wiped out if humankind is to continue. On the level of the individual criminal, however, he believes that the death penalty serves no purpose other than to dehumanize the society that inflicts it, and to turn the criminal's victims into victimizers themselves.

Much of Styron's fiction dwells on the process by which victims become victimizers. Nat Turner converts many of his fellow slaves from their turn-the-other-cheek Christianity to Old Testament end-of-the-world prophecy, with the result that scores of innocent people are slain, white and black alike. His reasons for rebellion are ample and sound, given the nature of slavery, but Styron nonetheless questions Nat's particular motivation and the means of this rebellion. Treated like Fortune's darling from birth, Nat converts his social superiority to a moral superiority and assumes a mandate from God to set the world to rights. The fact that Nat is a black man, and slavery the human institution in question, has thrown an emotional smoke screen over the issues at hand. In fact, Styron's conception of Nat's failings is very similar to his analysis of Helen Loftis in *Lie Down in Darkness*. Helen has been pampered by her father, Blood and Jesus Peyton, who saw the truth and acted upon it and taught his daughter in turn to stick to unyielding concepts of right and wrong, good and evil. Victimized to some extent by her marriage to the weak Milton Loftis, Helen perpetrates great crimes in the name of moral superiority; her own minister is chilled by the passion of hate that animates her, and by the damage she has wreaked on husband and child. In *Set This House on Fire*, Cass Kinsolving takes the law into his own hands and appropriates for himself the right to destroy Mason Flagg; that Flagg is innocent in the technical sense of murder is ultimately beside the point—as a human being he has the right to live. And so it goes, with character after character seeking and taking vengeance for crimes committed against them, and for limits set to their freedom.

Styron defines freedom as life's highest goal. He recognizes that not everyone seeks freedom, for freedom brings with it the burden of choice and acceptance of responsibility for choices made. Understandably, Nat Turner is frightened at first by his master's promise to release him: circumscribed lives mean circumscribed duties. Cass Kinsolving lives a life of voluntary imprisonment, in servitude to his alcoholism and Mason Flagg, precisely in order to evade taking care of himself and his family. After throwing Flagg off the cliff, he begs Luigi to cast him into prison, but Luigi refuses to allow his friend to wallow in self-pity any further, and releases him into a condition of freedom. Even in prison, however, humans have a certain degree of freedom that allows, indeed demands, the making of choices. People are not, after all, the flies on the wall that Nat Turner muses on, driven by instinct alone. However circumscribed one's life, however victimized one is by circumstances, there are certain pockets of freedom in which the exercise of individual will is possible. Within the parameters of military service, Captain Al Mannix chooses to carry out the order to march thirty-six miles in such a way that he flouts authority and asserts his fitness as a soldier both at the same time. Schwartz risks reprimand by his military superiors, the doctors in the clap shack, and steals a book that might set his friend Magruder free from ignorance and hence from tyranny. Sophie is faced with an impossible choice by the Auschwitz doctor, but it is a choice nonetheless, only one of many choices she will be faced with in the concentration camp. However determined the lives of Styron's characters seem to be—Milton Loftis, for example, continually complains that he has had no free will—there is always the necessity for choice. At Mai Lai and Auschwitz, in Port Warwick and Sambuco, everywhere there is the opportunity and necessity for choice.

The exercise of individual will often results in rebellion against the powers that would limit human freedom. Some of Styron's characters are too weak to rebel openly, so they take to drink (alcohol is a favorite Styron opiate, which lends a rosy glow to a drab and depressing world): these include Milton and Peyton Loftis, Cass Kinsolving, and Sophie. For Peyton and Sophie, only suicide provides permanent release. Other characters, as already mentioned, have the strength for revolt. If the revolt seems a "rebellion in reverse," like Mannix's, or ultimately self-defeating, like Nat Turner's, it is nonetheless understandable and even valuable when undertaken to correct what Styron considers evil: total domination of humans by other humans.

One of the epigrams to *Sophie's Choice* reads, "I seek that essential region of the soul where absolute evil confronts brotherhood." This region is literalized in the novel at the Auschwitz train station, when the doctor, who personifies total domination, faces Sophie and her two small children, a family symbolic of brotherhood. In that region, Styron says, "humanity is at its most mysterious."[9] Who shall live and who shall die in this confrontation? Most frequently, in the confrontation between evil and good, good perishes; but not always. It is instructive to look back on this point to *Set This House on Fire*, which Styron in 1972 said he preferred over his other three novels because, although less perfectly formed than they, "it has some of my most passionate and best stuff."[10] In certain ways, *Set This House on Fire* is a working through of the issues that inform *Sophie's Choice*. Certainly there are parallels in character portrayal: Peter Leverett and Stingo, drawn into the main characters' lives as both observers and participants; Celia and Sophie, battered mates whose love permits and encourages abuse; and, most importantly, Mason and Nathan, extravagant, wildly funny, living at the edge (in fact, the Washington hotel clerk tells Stingo that Sophie has called someone named "Mason. . . . Something like that").

When Stingo leaves *Set This House on Fire* out of the catalog of novels he contemplates writing, the reason is because he hasn't yet gone to Italy to have the experiences that make up the body of that novel (not because he's forgotten about it, as one critic states[11]); but the omission is in a certain sense a red flag, drawing attention to the earlier novel. That novel is a psychomachy—a war within the soul. Mason personifies the evil of which Cass is capable (and culpable), and Francesca Ricci personifies the brotherhood with which he would sustain himself. Having opted to attempt the release of the Riccis from pain and suffering, Cass finally rids himself of Mason Flagg's domination. Their final confrontation, in this allegorical interpretation, results in the triumph of good over evil.

Very few people live their lives in potentially deadly confrontations between good and evil. Most never put their lives on the line at all, preferring to lead safe, sane, ordinary existences somewhere nearer to the center than to the edge. Styron, however, is fascinated by those who live at the edge, whether by choice or circumstance, singed and ultimately consumed by the fires of lust, rage, hatred, jealousy, or a number of other overwhelming emotions. Although he recognizes the dangers of lives so lived, he seems energized by those lives and excited by their possibilities for moral instructiveness. Nat Turner, Nathan Landau, and Mason Flagg, among others, are larger than life, uncontainable by the straitjacket existences their society offers; as larger than life figures they are both better and worse than the mainstream, and instructive on both counts. Nat's passion for freedom, Nathan's hatred of Nazism, and Mason's desire for sexual liberation are all positive qualities. If these qualities are perverted by their possessors' single-minded madness, they nevertheless remain unconsumed by the flames that destroy the characters; instead they are refined and crystallized in the crucible of experience.

It has been said that Styron has a "Gothic taste for violence."[12] This categorization is usually leveled as a charge rather than stated as a description, as if it were a tasteless shortcoming —literary and otherwise—to write about beatings, stabbings, rape, suicide, and murder. But it should be remembered that the

Gothic novel flourished during the so-called Age of Enlighten-
ment, in the late eighteenth century, when artists gave voice to
the irrational urges that lay beneath the veneer of reason and
sanity in an era that stressed the rational and the sane. So, too,
Styron's Gothic taste for violence leads him to portray the pene-
tration into our modern technological age of passionate emotions that the age would repress. Those works written or set in
the late 1940s and 1950s express irrepressible, antisocial urges
seething in a conformist society. *The Confessions of Nat Turner*,
written in the 1960s, reveals the passion and turmoil of that
decade as well as of the 1830s. When one finally shuts the pages
on a Styron novel, when the murder and mayhem are over and
one's pulse stops racing, there is much to reflect upon coolly and
dispassionately; there are lessons to be learned about passionate
engagement in the struggle for liberation, about commitment,
daring, and risk.

To filter the intense experiences of his characters at the edge,
and to convey his moral messages, Styron frequently uses a
partially disengaged narrator whose own life is changed—presumably for the better—by participating in the cataclysmic events
of the story. Peter Leverett and Stingo are just such narrators,
recounting the events of the novels in the first person; Tom
Culver is another such figure, although he functions as what
Henry James called a "central intelligence" rather than a first-
person narrator (the novella is told in the third person). Each of
these characters finds his view of life altered by his friendship
with the central figures; in his struggle to understand the "other" he comes to understand himself better. In the process, innocent illusions are shed, and a deep sadness redeemed by occasional joy replaces the facile optimism that prevailed in the past.

This overarching sadness often makes William Styron emotionally demanding reading. Plowing through incident after incident of perversion, degradation, and despair, one finds the spirit
sinking. The reader begins to take on Cass Kinsolving's view of
humankind as a dying dog ceaselessly beaten with a stick, or as
a scrawny peasant woman with a load of fagots too heavy for
bearing. With Nat Turner one watches Andrew and Tom engaged in the repetitive task of moving sawhorses back and forth,

and the reader, too, takes the scene as emblematic of the "absurd and immemorial futility" of life. In his "Letter to an Editor," published in the first *Paris Review*, Styron maintains "that the times get precisely the literature that they deserve, and that if the writing of this period is gloomy the gloom is not as much inherent in the literature as in the times."[13]

Styron's narrative technique increases the all-pervasive gloom of his fiction. The climactic moments of his stories have already taken place before the stories begin—Peyton's suicide, Mason's murder, Nat's rebellion, Sophie's choice—and the narrators, recollecting the events leading up to these moments, often speak in portentous terms, creating a sense of impending doom. The danger of such a recollective mode is that the doom may seem trumped up, of the "had I only known what horrors awaited me" variety; and, in fact, Styron does not always avoid this danger successfully, especially in *Set This House on Fire*. The separate but related interior monologues of *Lie Down in Darkness* are perhaps Styron's most dramatic and successful means of conveying a feeling of inevitable catastrophe, since they reveal the characters working at cross purposes and therefore helping to "seal their fates." The Reverend Carey Carr, involved as Helen's confidant but detached from the central agonies, is a much more effective Greek chorus than anyone in *Set This House on Fire*, especially the lisping innkeeper Fausto Windgasser, who is not only marginal to the story but whose bathetic analogies of the events to "Gweek twagedy" are a bit obvious, not to mention comical.

Styron's tragedies are societal as well as domestic, collective as well as personal, global as well as local. They contain a "knife-blade of nostalgia" not only for the rural South, but for the moral clarity that always seems to have animated the era just before one's own, where good was good and evil was evil, and the choices between them clear. The father figures in Styron's works often speak with moral certainty, but the sons and daughters are lost and floundering, expelled from Eden. Styron began to write his first novel not long after 1945, a date to which some assign the fall of the modern world, with the explosion of nuclear bombs and the discovery of the existence of Auschwitz. The "good" side dropped those bombs; ordinary men doing their duty helped to perpetuate the concentration camps. It is not only the "latent capacity for rage and disorder" that one must fear, as Stingo characterizes Nathan, and as wells out of Mason Flagg, but also the reasoned and determined search for order at all costs. It is dangerous for one to maintain one's delusions that Eden, a simpler age, still exists—to ask, as Morris Fink does in 1947, "What's Owswitch?"

After speaking in his *Paris Review* letter of the gloom inherent in the times, Styron goes on to note that the writer cannot refuse to bear witness to this gloom: "he *must* go on writing, reflecting disorder, defeat, despair, should that be all he sees at the moment, but ever searching for the elusive love, joy, and hope—qualities which . . . are best when they have to be struggled for, and are not commonly come by with much ease."[14] It is the occasional moment of union or brotherhood, sexual or otherwise, toward which Styron would have us aspire, not a union of esprit de corps bonding, in bureaucracies that sacrifice the individual on the alter of the group, but rather fellow feeling of the sort that creates and nourishes friendship. Brotherhood in Styron's novels is rarely shown as obtaining in the group situation, whether the group is the family, the military unit, the nation, race, or religion. Certainly family life is domestic hell on earth: Peyton and Maudie are unwilling and even unwitting antagonists, pitted against each other by virtue of their parents' battle. The melting-pot nature of the marines on the hospital ward does not ensure empathy with others, as *In the Clap Shack* reveals. Sharing blackness or Protestantism or a German heritage cannot guarantee union. Everywhere on the level of the group there is division and divisiveness.

Brotherhood as Styron finds it operates most successfully on the level of the twosome (in the case of *Sophie's Choice*, a threesome), especially between two males. Wherever one looks in Styron's fiction one finds two males bonding, often because of their mutual undertaking of a test by fire. Harry Miller and Lennie, their friendship initiated when Harry saves Lennie's life; Nat Turner and Hark, their own comradeship forged through the slave's deprivation of family life and strengthened by revolu-

tion; Tom Culver and Al Mannix; Peter Leverett and Cass Kinsolving—all of these brother relationships fill a void in the characters' lives and stem, perhaps, from their creator's deeply felt
need, as an only child, for a soulmate.

In contrast to these vivid male friendships, Styron's hetero-
sexual relationships are less convincing. Many of his female
characters seem to be unreal, more like ideas than people. If
Rosemarie Laframboise is intended by the author to be Mason
Flagg's "bimbo," an object of desire for Mason to flaunt like his
red cadillac, then it must be noted with sadness that too many
other Styron females are closer to representations than to flesh-
and-blood people. Margaret Whitehead, Poppy Kinsolving,
Francesca Ricci, even Sophie seem to be figments of the male
imagination, either the male characters' or the author's. In the
extreme view, Sophie is only a male fantasy in a rite-of-passage
story.[15] Certainly, Styron's women are not totally unilateral: if
Poppy is angel she is also earth mother; if Francesca Ricci and
Margaret Whitehead are sex objects they are also catalysts for
moral regeneration. Nonetheless, even so complex a character as
Sophie seems to be a projection or shadowy phantom rather
than a real person. Peyton Loftis is more convincing, perhaps
because she intentionally exists as a phantom for most of the
novel, a part of the mere recollections and musings of the other
characters. When she is finally met directly, portrayed through
interior monologue, she appears starkly real by contrast to her
earlier incarnations (indeed, all of the characters whose minds
are penetrated in *Lie Down in Darkness* attain the roundness of
fully developed characters). But Sophie, for all her power and
force, is problematic. Even if one believes in her as a person, her
sexual nature has many qualities of the postpubescent wish-
fulfillment variety: Stingo's appropriately, Styron's less so. Her
orgiastic couplings, first with Nathan and then (paradise at last!)
with Stingo, are arguably off target. At least one critic, Robert
Alter, contends that by exercising the full prerogatives of the new
sexual candor, Styron has compromised his novel artistically. In
Alter's view, Stingo's achievement of his sexual goal is "more a
beautiful masturbatory fantasy than a credible novelistic scene.
With a little ingenuity, of course, one might find a 'symbolic'

justification, but the tenor of the scene, and of others like it, seems all wrong."[16]

The "symbolic justification" for this scene and others like it hinges on Styron's view of sex as expressed throughout his career. Growing up in the thirties and forties in the American South, Styron was enmeshed in a sexually repressive culture. As a consequence, he views sex in most instances as a destructive rather than a constructive force; pushed down by society, the sexual urge rises to express itself in perverse ways. Nat Turner's revolutionary impulse, as Styron sees it, stems in part from sublimated and rechanneled sexual desire. Mason Flagg, searching for ways to flout society and give vent to his strong masculinity (in his view), indulges himself in pornography. Dr. Glanz, in his clap shack, takes voyeuristic and salacious pleasure from his patients' sexual activities, exploiting their private lives in the name of healing. Peyton Loftis's adolescent confusion over her own sexual nature, her father's adultery, and her mother's prudishness helps to drive her into promiscuity and the inability to love. Leslie Lapidus and Mary Alice Grimball have liberated themselves only to the extent of performing symbolic sex acts, and tease poor Stingo to the brink of despair. Masquerading as religious salvation or artistic freedom or medical matter or Freudian chic, sex is only rarely a life force in Styron's view. It is against such a background, in *Sophie's Choice* as well as the works that precede it, that Sophie's joyful lovemaking must be set. Writing his novel in the sexually liberated 1970s, Styron created a heroine whose sexual creativeness bears the weight of the 1940s postwar generation, struggling to forget the horrors of Auschwitz and to assert the power of life over the power of death.

It is because *Sophie's Choice* is more nearly Stingo's story than Sophie's that questions of the "appropriateness" of its sexual episodes might be put to rest. As is often the case with Styron, a large "meaningful theme"—the creation and maintaining of concentration camps—combines with a smaller one—the coming to maturity of the artist—to create the sense that one is reading more than one book at once. So, too, Styron refers to the dropping of the atomic bomb on Nagasaki to give larger significance to the decline of the Loftises in *Lie Down in Darkness*, and relates the agonies of *Set This House on Fire* to American material- ism. In all three cases, critics have taken issue with the mixing of subject matters, finding them at artistic cross purposes at times. A similar problem is evident with respect to *The Confessions of Nat Turner*. In his desire to portray slavery from the inside, getting at what it must have been like to be a slave in Virginia in the 1830s, and in an effort to free himself from his own racial prejudices as a white Southerner, Styron has taken a real-life personage and told his story. The violent reaction to the novel by many readers, especially blacks, centers on the right of a white man to "appro- priate" a black hero and to provide him with problematic motiva- tion for action.

A headline in one newspaper following the awarding of the Pulitzer Prize to *The Confessions of Nat Turner* was "Bill Styron's 'Catching It' over 'Turner Confessions'."[17] Styron's been "catch- ing it" over this novel for years. Controversy has stemmed large- ly from the racial issue, the main bone of contention being the alleged distortion or suppression of the facts, resulting in a por- trait of Nat Turner very unlike the original. Although the book reveals Styron's own sensibility, his own world view, Styron firmly believes—and many agree—that it reveals the spirit of slavery as well.[18] Furthermore, in its focus on, and examination of, a historical period, the novel speaks about freedom and dom- ination as the quintessential struggle of humankind, cutting across race, class, and era. As Styron remarked in his acceptance speech for the Howells Medal:

a novel can possess a significance apart from its subject matter and . . . the story of a nineteenth-century black slave may try to say at least as much about longing, loneliness, personal betrayal, madness, and the quest for God as it does about Negroes or the institution of slavery.[19]

The critical reception to this book as well as to Styron's other novels has on the whole been more favorable abroad, especially in France, than in the United States. Europeans seem to have less trouble than Americans with the imaginative liberties that

Styron, as historical novelist, has taken with the facts. Styron feels better understood in France than perhaps anywhere else, crediting the French with a true appreciation of and respect for the creative writer as a powerful force for good in society. In addition, Styron considers Europeans to be more fully aware than Americans of large historical forces that, if not acknowledged, can overwhelm any human being at any time. One impetus for the creation of *Sophie's Choice*—tellingly subtitled *A Memory* in its original version—was the question posed by a television talk-show host to a group of mostly non-Jewish investigators into Nazism: why should gentiles be concerned about or interested in the Holocaust? To Styron, the question was "very close to indecent. I could not help thinking whether there was something paradigmatically American (or certainly non-European) in that question, with its absence of any sense of history and its vacuous unawareness of evil."[20] The education in evil that the innocent American, Stingo, receives from the experienced European, Sophie, is necessary, not only for his growth as a human being but also, presumably, for his growth as an artist. Armed with his knowledge, the imagination to present this knowledge in a compelling way, and the freedom to explore territories alien to his own experience, the artist becomes what Shelley called the legislator of the world. Styron would undoubtedly agree with Shelley that "the great instrument of moral good is the imagination."

Flannery O'Connor, another southern writer in the "Gothic" mode, has recorded a remark made to her by Maurice Coindreau, the French translator she shared with Styron, that in the view of the French, Styron was "the greatest thing since Faulkner."[21] That comparisons with Faulkner are double-edged was well known by O'Connor herself, who once stated that nobody likes to get caught on the tracks when the Dixie Special comes through. Contemporary southern writers resist comparisons with the acknowledged southern master of fiction, for fear of being diminished by the aggrandizement. Certainly Styron himself was influenced by Faulkner, among others, whose works he steeped himself in during the 1940s. He explained in the French journal *Le Monde* that "You cannot become a writer with-

out falling under influences and being affected by them, in order
to create a universe in your image. The shadow of Faulkner
glides over my first works, but no responsible critic can say that I
am a disciple of Faulkner. I am my own master."[22]

The presence of Faulkner might arguably be considered a bit
more than a shadow in *Lie Down in Darkness*, with its parallels to
Faulkner's characters, jumbled time sequences, narrative struc-
tures, and plot devices. Nevertheless, Styron has always been
his own master.[23] His literary debts, especially in the earlier
works, are clear to any serious reader of fiction: stream-of-con-
sciousness technique from Faulkner and Joyce; crime-and-pun-
ishment theme from Sophocles and Dostoevsky; rags-to-riches
motif and detached narrator from Fitzgerald; grand, orotund
prose style from Wolfe; emphasis on the craft of fiction from
Flaubert. But Styron has never hidden these debts. He fully
acknowledges his teachers in interviews, in Stingo's list of reading materials, in essays collected in *This Quiet Dust* and grouped
together under the title "Forebears." In spite of the echoes from
earlier writers, Styron's works have always been daring and
original, and indubitably his own. At times they suffer from
certain excesses—looseness of plot, hyperventilation of emotions, a gratuitously polysyllabic vocabulary, an overabundance
of words, words, words. Sometimes his reach toward what
Melville called the mighty theme is greater than his grasp, and
the theme itself, because of the failure of grasp, seems grandiose
rather than grand. The same criticisms, no doubt, have been
leveled at some of Styron's acknowledged masters, and they do
not detract from the richness and importance of Styron's literary
career. His passion and humanity mark him as one of America's
best modern writers, whose painstaking dedication to the craft
of fiction and the "meaningful theme" has produced fiction of
lasting consequence.

Afterword:
William Styron in the
Kingdom of the Jews*

One of the more comical passages in *Sophie's Choice* concerns
Stingo's early misconceptions about the religious practices of the
Jew. As an eleven-year-old Virginian Presbyterian, staring from
his churchyard at Congregation Rodef Sholem across the street,
Stingo imagines "the rabbis in skullcaps moaning in a guttural
tongue as they [go] about their savage rites—circumcising goats,
burning oxen, disemboweling newborn lambs." Years later, a
not-much-wiser Stingo finds the tables turned—*he* is the quaint
and often misunderstood outsider, stranger in a strange land,
Southerner in the North, gentile in Brooklyn's kingdom of the
Jews. Even though neither Stingo nor Sophie is a Jew, and even
though an important impetus for Styron's writing the novel was
to indicate that the Holocaust was not the sole province of the
Jews,[1] *Sophie's Choice* is so very much concerned with the Jewish
experience that it would seem naturally to generate curiosity
about Styron's interest in Jewish material.

A few readers, Jews especially, have faulted Styron for creating a Christian heroine as victim of Nazi persecution; but on the
whole the storm of protest that Styron anticipated, having been
burned in this regard by the publication of *Nat Turner*, never
materialized. In fact, readers have paid little attention to Styron's
treatment of Jewish-Christian relations, and, so far as I know,
critics have rarely focused on Styron's lifelong fascination with
the Jew. The one work on the subject is less than adequate.

*A paper originally presented at the Seventh Winthrop Symposium on
Major Modern Writers, "William Styron: Novelist and Public Figure,"
Winthrop College, Rock Hill, South Carolina, April 1986.

Entitled "Bellow, Malamud, Roth. . . . . . . and Styron? or One Jewish Writer's Response," this article, by Irving Saposnik, considers only three of Styron's characters—Harry Miller, Al Mannix, and Nathan Landau—and then only as suffering victims.[2] It ignores two of Styron's most important Jewish-American characters—Slotkin in *Set This House on Fire* and Schwartz in *In the Clap Shack*—not to mention the Old Testament Jews in *The Confessions of Nat Turner*, whom Styron subtly Americanizes.

My purpose is to gauge the nature and extent of one of Styron's major interests with reference to the full range of his major fiction as well as to his biography. To set the interest in context I begin with a brief glance at the history of the portrayal of the Jew in the works of other non-Jewish American writers.

In the nineteenth century, the Jew appeared in the literature of such well-known Christians as Longfellow, Melville, and Hawthorne, sometimes in a neutral or favorable light, as in Longfellow's poem on the Jewish cemetery at Newport, or in Melville's *Clarel*, sometimes most unfavorably, as in Hawthorne's *English Notebooks*. Often an author portrayed the Jew with admiration in one piece, with repugnance in another, and even expressed this ambivalence within a single work. Stock motifs commonly employed in this period include the Wandering Jew, the conversion of the Jews, Jews and money, Jews as an ancient people. References to the contemporary Jew are infrequent, undoubtedly because Jews were small in number in America until the great waves of immigration from Germany in mid-century and from Eastern Europe a few decades later.

Just after World War I and the end of that second wave, the Jewish character became mythically viable in this country, often in a grossly anti-Semitic fashion, as Gentiles anxious to resist the Jewish attempts at incorporation into the American mainstream created caricatures of the Jew as pseudoartist and grasping materialist. The emergence of this fictional cliché resulted, some surmise, from the movement of provincial writers like Dreiser, Anderson, and Wolfe to the big cities, where they discovered that the Jew had beaten them to the artists' quarters; other provincials, attempting expatriation—Hemingway, Pound, Eliot, Fitzgerald, and Cummings, for example—found Jews vexingly pres-

ent even on the Left Bank. Their subsequent portrayal of the
Jew ran the narrow gamut from Wolfe's Jewesses stinking of rut
and crotch to Eliot's "jew" squatting on the windowsill. To be
sure, some non-Jewish writers—including Sinclair Lewis, John
Dos Passos, John Hersey, and Richard Wright—treated the Jew
sympathetically, but the negative attitude of others was scathingly summarized in a 1930 article reviewing the fictional use of
Jews in the preceding decade: "For these writers [Robert Her-
rick, Willa Cather, Ernest Hemingway, Edith Wharton] [the Jew]
is a symbol of modern social disintegration. Here, they say in
effect, is what our subtle and discriminating Anglo-Saxon culture has come to—this contact with a type that is influencing and
yet can never understand our values."[3]

But after the next war, the Jew became a spokesman for
modern life as it had begun to appear to many American intellectuals—a life of dislocation, alienation, and exile; and the Jewish
writer's creation of a literature of marginality (a la Bellow's dan-
gling man) began to be seen as an articulation of universally felt
emotions and situations. William Styron began to write at this
time. I believe that it is in this context of outsidedness and
marginality rather than of victimization per se that Styron's Jewish characters are most profitably set.

Stingo's aforementioned childish musings on the Jews indicate the alien nature of this tiny religious minority in the small
town of the South. But as the child of a very liberal father for his
time and place, and as a student at Duke University in the mid-
1940s, which then as now attracted many northern Jews, William
Styron early developed not only a tolerance but even a predilection for persons of the Jewish persuasion. His friendships at
Duke, and at Davidson before that, were, if not exclusively, then
primarily with Jews; as he would later explain, he simply got
along better with them than he did with non-Jews. Feeding this
predilection was an *in*tolerance for institutionalized Christianity
as he observed it, especially as practiced by the rootless country-
club suburbanites pictured in his first novel. "I think that I have
a hypersensitivity to Waspdom," Styron confessed to Raymond
Sokolov in 1967. "I mean, really a hypersensitivity, like exacer-
bated nerves."[4] Congenitally rebellious it seems—indeed, after his

mother's death, Styron was sent away to prep school because of his intractability—Styron consciously rebelled from the mores of his small-town life by sympathizing with non-Wasps; like his protagonist in *Lie Down in Darkness*, William Styron even married a Jewish artist, although this union has proved more lasting than Peyton's. Of Rose Burgunder Styron has noted, only half joking-ly, "She's my Jewish mama. She's very beautiful, and I would have married her anyway—but she happens to be Jewish. And not many boys from Virginia do that."[5]

The casual to virulent anti-Semitism of the Virginia society in which Styron was raised is well evidenced in *Lie Down in Darkness*. Mrs. La Farge, for example, blames the international Jewish bankers for World War II. Although the guests at Peyton's wedding accept Harry Miller as "the better kind" (only on the basis of Peyton's having chosen him), Helen Loftis views this choice of bridegroom as evidence of her daughter's moral degra-dation as well as Peyton's slap in her mother's face by bringing a mongrel Jew into this proper Virginia household. Union with Harry provides Styron a shorthand way of indicating Peyton's rebellion and potential salvation from a stultifying society. As unconvincing a character as Harry Miller may appear to some, he is a well-constructed emblem of the good, the true, and the just. Though Styron's conception of Peyton changed from the early version of the novel, called *Inheritance of Night* (the name it bears in *Sophie's Choice*), in which she is a grasping, venal wom-an, his conception of this Jew as moral touchstone remained constant from first to last.[6] Harry Miller as Jew and especially as Jewish artist testifies to tragedy but refuses to capitulate to it; like Bellow's Herzog a decade later, he sees the wasteland but re-nounces the wasteland mentality, opting instead for life and hope.

When he was writing *Lie Down in Darkness*, after graduation from Duke, Styron shared an off-Broadway apartment with a Jewish friend and through him got "the smell of this urban Jew-ish life, and loved it." All of Styron's best friends at this time were Jews. Shortly after completing his first novel he was called into the marines and trained at Camp Lejeune in North Caro-lina, undergoing the long march that gave his next work its title.

No actual Captain Mannix type populated this corps of reservists, but there *was* one large Jewish haberdasher from North Carolina who complained a great deal, and he became the model for Mannix. How real people "become" fictional characters is a fascinating and complex study in itself, not even to be approached here; but perhaps I might be permitted to surmise that Styron's philo-Semitism predisposed him toward transmuting one griping Jewish haberdasher into a rebel of heroic proportions, engaged in an entirely fictional conflict with the military bureaucracy. Styron supports this view, having described Culver, the novella's central consciousness, as "a kind of archetypal WASP, who has a fantastic admiration for this Jew. . . . There's nothing contrived about it. . . . It just comes out of my nature."[7] Whether Mannix is hero or madman (Mannix/manic) may be, and has been, debated—perhaps he is both. Certainly he is the Jew as outsider and rebel against a society that would stifle creativity, delay maturity, and snuff out individuality. In his own way, Mannix is an artist, creating out of the givens of his society—Templeton's order to march—an original, daring and ultimately prescriptive mode of behavior.

In Styron's next work of fiction, *Set This House on Fire*, a Jew once again acts as a clear moral touchstone in a novel whose convoluted narrative structure mirrors the confusion of values in modern society. This Jew is not a character in the novel as much as he is a recollection by Cass Kinsolving, a tendency in Kinsolving's personality that must be fully credited and acted upon before he can become what the Jews call a *Mensch*, or a worthwhile human being. Captain Slotkin, a Jew from Brookline, Massachusetts, is the navy psychiatrist who treats Kinsolving during a wartime episode of mental illness. He shares with this southern Methodist from Lake Waccamaw, North Carolina, a religious upbringing grounded in Isaiah and Job, and this Old Testament heritage forges a link between them. In the course of treatment, Slotkin gives Kinsolving a copy of *Complete Greek Plays* and advises his patient to heed the lessons taught by the great playwrights. Echoes of the Oedipus tragedies reverberate throughout the novel, and even in Kinsolving's depths of degradation and despair he recalls Slotkin's advice to follow Oedipus's example in rising above tragic events. "He seemed to make so much natural and gentle, decent sense that I almost gave in to the bastard," Kinsolving muses about Slotkin. In this novel about the search for a sustaining faith, it is to Slotkin that Kinsolving the orphan and apostate prays: "Slotkin old father, old rabbi, what shall I do? Teach me now in my need." Eventually another wise counselor, Luigi the cop, completes the task that Slotkin had begun years before. Though suffering in itself does not lead to grace—indeed, Luigi complains that Kinsolving sins in his suffering—Styron suggests that suffering is sometimes necessary to turn people from "smug contented hogs" rooting at the trough of shallow materialism and pseudoart into human beings with minds and hearts and souls. Behind this concept implicitly stands the suffering Jew, not as victim, but rather as one who is emboldened by his pain into action for others, and who, like Slotkin, testifies to the dignity of man and the power of life.

In his one attempt at playwriting, *In the Clap Shack*, Styron deliberately focuses on the Jew as suffering victim but also as rebel.[8] Once again the actual protagonist is a Southerner: Wally Magruder is a younger, more naive version of Tom Culver or Peter Leverett, in fact a version of Styron himself, who as a raw recruit was likewise mistakenly incarcerated on a venereal ward ("segregated like Jews in a ghetto," he calls it[9]) for a case of syphilis that turned out to be trench mouth. Like much fiction of World War II, Styron's play is populated by a variety of ethnic types: one Italian, one Irishman, one black, one Jew, and so forth. The convention of the sensitive Jew in the United States Army, popularized by works of Jews like Norman Mailer and Irwin Shaw and turned on its head by Philip Roth (in his short story, "Defender of the Faith"), is closely followed in Styron's play, created in the early 1970s at the height of public recognition of Jewish-American literature.

Although Wally Magruder is the hero, like Cass Kinsolving he receives moral instruction from a Jew, a solemn, bespectacled, older man (hence rabbinical in looks) suffering from renal tuberculosis (a "Jewish" disease). Schwartz in turn receives instruction from a book called *Tolerance for Others, or How to Develop Human Compassion*, written by a rabbi from none other than Congregation Rodef Sholem, where Stingo once thought goats were circumcised and oxen burned. The book's thesis is that since the Jews have endured so much suffering they must empathize with other sufferers and be the standard bearers in the march for human compassion. Undeniably Schwartz's so-called Jewish compassion is arrogant as well as naive and misleading, allowing him to humanize the monstrous Dr. Glanz. Schwartz is more problematical a "rabbi" than Slotkin, then, for Styron shows us his foibles and weaknesses. Although Schwartz doesn't like to use the word *nigger*, when a black patient verbally assaults him as a Jew-boy he is quick to call him a *Schwarze*, the Yiddish equivalent of *nigger*; his own Schwartzness, or condition of being the hated other, does not automatically link them or lead to tolerance. Nonetheless, like Slotkin and his offering of the Greek plays, Schwartz and his advice from *Tolerance for Others* serve as moral touchstones in this play. Indeed, Styron highlighted this book in his revised version of *In the Clap Shack*, in the crucial death scene between Clark, the black man, and Schwartz. Whereas in the first version "some sort of funny revelation" comes to Schwartz, leading him to understand Clark and reach out to him, in the final version Schwartz gets his insights only after looking into Rabbi Weinberg's book.[10] Its ethical modes of conduct are then felt and acted upon rather than merely read; Styron suggests that Schwartz does gain from this rabbi the courage to embrace a "brother" who refuses his overtures to the bitter end. Reinforcing the notion that the Jews are people of the Book, whose religion is one of action rather than creed, Styron has Schwartz steal a medical book for Wally Magruder, so that both men may flout the society that imprisons them.

Shortly before publication of *The Confessions of Nat Turner*, Styron confided to Raymond Sokolov, "I never sought to idealize, for instance, Jews or Negroes because they were Jews or Negroes. I just tried to find [a] . . . balancing opposite, which satisfied something that I need."[11] Having long felt a moral imperative to come to know the black man, Styron created *The Confessions of Nat Turner* after a lifetime of searching for rapprochement. Set in Virginia in the 1830s, the novel takes to task the various Christian denominations whose uncompassionate creeds and practices created and sustained a black slave society. The Reverend Richard Whitehead's Methodist sermon to the "darkies," quoting scripture to keep them docile and in their place (based on an actual sermon of the period); the traveling Episcopal ministers, justifying slavery as God's intention; the Baptist Reverend Alexander Eppes, engaging in perverse religious exaltations while degrading his slave Nat—to Styron, all these men of the cloth behave in a decidedly unchristian fashion. Although actual Jews are absent from the small towns in which the events of the novel occur, Nat Turner takes his inspiration for rebellion from the Old Testament prophets urging moral regeneration. He views the blacks in his community as particularly akin to the Jews described in Exodus, sharing names like Nathan and Joseph as well as the state of being persecuted and victimized. By following Moses, Nat tells his followers, in words they can understand, "them Jewish peoples they could stand up an' live like *men*. They became a great nation. No more fatback, no more pint of salt, no more peck of corn fo' them Jews; no more overseers, no more auction blocks; no more horn blow at sunrise fo' them mothahs' sons. They had chicken with pot likker an' spoonbread an' sweet cider to drink in the shade. They done got paid an honest dollar. Them Jews become *men*." Although Styron has stated that *The Confessions of Nat Turner* is about Old Testament vengeance redeemed by New Testament charity,[12] the New Testament salvation seems to me the most trumped-up and least convincing religious element in the novel. What one remembers as the moral imperative is Nat Turner's desire for rebellion from an oppressive white society, a moral imperative well expressed by the flight of the Jews from Egypt and by Styron's implied identification of the blacks and the Jews.

My brief foray through Styron's fiction brings us finally to Styron's best-known work after *The Confessions of Nat Turner*: *Sophie's Choice*. A fascinating sidelight on Styron's lifelong fictional use of Jews is found in some unaccessioned materials housed at Duke University, three holograph pages that were probably intended for inclusion in *Sophie's Choice* and later rejected by the author as "inappropriate" and "far-fetched" for that novel.[13] In them, a first-person narrator attributes his feeling of rootlessness and lack of identification as a Southerner to the fact that, although raised as a Presbyterian, he is really a Jew. He discovers in his father's papers, after the old man's death, a family tree that identifies one of his remote ancestors as an eighteenth-century rabbi, one Baruch Levi, who established a synagogue in South Carolina. To the narrator, this discovery means that he is "at least half a Jew." That the narrator claims half-Jewishness on the basis of blood so thinned by the passage of centuries, and that the force of this blood is great enough in his mind to account for his sense of not belonging, are surely significant facts. Indeed, the narrator states that adjustment to his newfound Jewishness is not difficult: "I went through a phase of sneaky, truculent anti-Semitism, which lasted until I was almost full-grown, and which was followed by a period in which I made a complete reversal, when all the devilish happenings in the world seemed to be the work of Christians." The manuscript ends here, leaving a tantalizing glimpse of Styron fantasizing himself as a Jew.

Sophie's Choice is, finally, Styron's one full-fledged Jewish book. The reason lies not in its Holocaust subject (again, not all victims of the concentration camps were Jews) or its Jewish characters (one modeled on the Jewish girls Styron knew at Duke[14]) in their Jewish setting (Yetta's Brooklyn pink palace, similar to the establishment Styron occupied in the 1940s and has called "a sort of Saul Bellow type boarding house"[15]). Rather, I think of *Sophie's Choice* as Jewish in flavor because of its characteristically Jewish style. Nathan Landau—that Jewish version of Mason Flagg, that madder version of Al Mannix—predicts the rise of the Jewish-American novel, and Styron has in fact woven the fabric of his own novel under instruction by those premier Jewish haberdashers, the Hart, Schaffner, and Marx of the Jewish novel: that is, Bellow, Malamud, and Roth.[16] So we come full circle back to Saposnik's article. But the great similarity between Styron's *Sophie's Choice* and the works of the three major Jewish-American authors is not, to me, in its concentration on the Jew as suffering victim or rebel, and certainly not as moral touchstone; rather, it is in the use of a certain tone passed down from Sholem Aleichem's Tevye to Bellow's Herzog. Self-deprecating and wry, alternatingly inflating and deflating, it is a comic mode adopted as a defense against tragedy.

In an interview of the early 1970s, Styron characterized the Jewish sensibility as "that comic awareness so exquisitely poised between hilarity and anguish."[17] He would soon adopt that sensibility as a perfect means of expressing not only the incomprehensible events at Auschwitz but also the passage made by Stingo from innocence to experience, on several levels; this sensibility is also a strategy for coping with all of those happenings. So the Leslie Lapidus episode is juxtaposed to Sophie's descent into hell, the two orders of experience setting each other off, the comic sexual fumblings heightening the tragic loss of personhood and relieving it at the same time. And within the sections and the sentences embodying Stingo's desperate attempts to lose his virginity, Styron uses an inflated rhetoric to match Stingo's hopes as well as his libido, coupled with a deflated rhetoric that mocks (but does not destroy) those hopes. Ogling the provocative Leslie Lapidus in her bathing suit, Stingo worships her astounding breasts and perfect navel, imagining the latter as a goblet brimming not with champagne but with lemon Kool-Aid. The unexpected presence of Kool-Aid in that sophisticated navel pulls the rug out from under Stingo's aspirations toward grandeur. Styron effectively uses a double rhythm in the concentration camp episodes, in which he contrasts Sophie's sublime agonies at Auschwitz with Stingo's ridiculous banana gorging in the States. More subtly, he contrasts Sophie's yearning toward her attic eyrie, "the celibate retreat of a calcimine purity," with the monosyllabically expressive reality of her existence in a cellar that "[stinks] of rot and mold."

Such a wry or ironic comic mode may come readily to a Southerner, regardless of his immersion in New York Jewish society or marriage to a Jew; for the Southerner like the Jew is often conscious of the burden of a tragic past. Walker Percy—whom Styron admires, by the way[18]—has stated his debt to Jewish humor, not merely because the phrase "Jewish comedian" is almost a tautology in modern American society but also because the Jews and a man of Percy's (and Styron's) temperament need a way to acknowledge the oppressiveness of life while affirming its possibilities.[19] With its comedy tinged with despair, its tragedy lightened by laughter, *Sophie's Choice* reveals Styron's kinship with the Jews in a more pronounced way than ever before. The Presbyterian from Newport News, Virginia, has indeed come to roost in the kingdom of the Jews.

Notes

1. REVOLUTIONARY WORKS IN AN ORDINARY LIFE

1. The biographical information in this chapter was gleaned primarily from the following sources: the bulk of the material comes from the William Styron Collection, Manuscript Department, Duke University Library, Durham, North Carolina, especially the three-volume scrapbook compiled by Styron's father and donated to Duke in 1961; an unpublished paper entitled "The Genesis of W. S.," written in 1951 by Styron's father for Bobbs-Merrill; an interview with Styron by Raymond Sokolov, portions of which were published in "Into the Mind of Nat Turner," *Newsweek* (October 16, 1967), pp. 65–69; and the manuscript of Styron's 1981 acceptance speech as Virginian of the year. Other important sources are essays in Styron's collection *This Quiet Dust*, most notably "This Quiet Dust," "The Oldest America," "Christchurch," "The James," "Almost a Rhodes Scholar," "Lie Down in Darkness," "The Paris Review," and "William Blackburn;" Georgann Eubanks, "William Styron: The Confessions of a Southern Writer," in *Conversations with William Styron*, ed. James L. W. West III (Jackson: University Press of Mississippi, 1985), pp. 265–75; Kevin Sack, "Duke's Choice," *Tobacco Road*, 4 (May 1981), pp. 6–8, 32; James W. West, "William Styron: A Biographical Account," *Mississippi Quarterly*, 34 (Winter 1980–81), pp. 2–7.
2. This handwriting analysis is found in volume 1 of his father's scrapbooks.
3. For a fictionalized account of Styron's experience at McGraw-Hill see "My Life as a Publisher," *Esquire* (March 14, 1978), pp. 71–79. This account was adapted from Styron's then-novel-in-progress, *Sophie's Choice*.
4. For a discussion of Styron's French reputation see Valarie M. Arms, "William Styron in France," in *Critical Essays on William Styron*, ed. Arthur D. Casciato and James L. W. West III (Boston: G. K. Hall & Co., 1982), pp. 306–15.
5. *William Styron's Nat Turner: Ten Black Writers Respond*, ed. John Henrik Clark (Boston: Beacon Press, 1968).

6. Information about the changing conception of *The Way of the War-rior* was gathered from Willie Morris, "About the Author: William Styron," *Book-of-the-Month Club News*, Midsummer 1979, p. 3; Mi-chiko Kakutani, "William Styron on His Life and Work," *New York Times Book Review*, December 12, 1982, p. 26; Georgann Eubanks, "William Styron: The Confessions of a Southern Writer," pp. 272–73; Philip Caputo, "Styron's Choices," *Esquire*, 106 (December 1986), pp. 156–59.

7. Walker Percy, "The Man on the Train," in *The Message in the Bottle: How Queer Man Is, How Queer Language Is, and What One Has to Do with the Other* (New York: Farrar, Straus and Giroux, 1978), p. 83.

2. A DREAM DENIED: *THE CONFESSIONS OF NAT TURNER*

1. This essay, collected in *This Quiet Dust*, is an invaluable source of information on *The Confessions of Nat Turner* in particular and Sty-ron's southern background in general.

2. See, for example, Vincent Harding, "You've Taken My Nat and Gone," in *William Styron's Nat Turner: Ten Black Writers Respond*, p. 25. This collection of essays also reprints Thomas Gray's "Confes-sions of Nat Turner," originally published in 1831.

3. Styron's annotated copy of Drewry's book is included in the Wil-liam Styron Collection, Perkins Library, Duke University. For addi-tional discussion of Styron's use of details about southern slave life from Drewry's *The Southampton Insurrection*, as well as Frederick Law Olmsted's *A Journey in the Seaboard Slave States*, see Arthur D. Casciato and James L. W. West III, "William Styron and *The South-ampton Insurrection*," in *Critical Essays on William Styron*, pp. 213–25.

4. C. Van Woodward and R. W. B. Lewis, "The Confessions of Wil-liam Styron," a transcript of a November 1967 radio program col-lected in *Conversations with William Styron*, p. 87.

5. In a footnote to "This Quiet Dust," p. 16, Styron points to Erik Erikson's *Young Man Luther* for the relationship of the revolutionary impulse to the father figure. He adds, "Although it is best to be wary of any heavy psychoanalytical emphasis, one cannot help believing that Nat Turner's relationship with his father (or his sur-rogate father, his master) was tormented and complicated, like Luther's."

6. "William Styron on *The Confessions of Nat Turner*: A *Yale Lit* Inter-

view," ed. Douglas Barzelay and Robert Sussman (1986), in *Conversations with William Styron*, p. 97.

7. The effect of Turner's rebellion on the institution of slavery was equally unhappy and ironic. Virginia, which had been moving toward emancipation, clamped down upon its black citizens, establishing laws to restrict their movement, assembly, and education.

8. For a discussion of Nat Turner and other Styron characters as solitary pursuers of individual dreams, see John Kenny Crane, *The Root of All Evil: The Thematic Unity of William Styron's Fiction* (Columbia: University of South Carolina Press, 1984).

9. Styron discusses the novel as a religious allegory in the Barzelay and Sussman interview, pp. 95–97.

3. IN SEARCH OF ORDER: *LIE DOWN IN DARKNESS*

1. So Styron told Jack Griffin et al. about his use of time in his fiction, in "A Conversation with William Styron," January 14, 1985, reprinted in *Conversations with William Styron*, p. 55.

2. Barry Maine of Wake Forest University discussed "William Styron's Newport News in *Lie Down in Darkness*" at a conference on Styron at Winthrop College, April 12, 1986, to which this paragraph is indebted.

3. In an earlier conception of *Lie Down in Darkness*, then called *Inheritance of Night*, Peyton is feral rather than simply troubled. Poor retarded Maudie commits suicide at age twenty-nine after being victimized all her life by her sister. Peyton tries to drown her own infant in the bath tub, takes up with a married man in order to seek vengeance on her father (who loves the man's wife), and persuades the married man's father, dying of cancer, to cut his own son (who, incidentally, loves Peyton) out of his will. Styron's outline, called *The Story of Peyton Loftis*, along with early drafts of the novel, is found in Box 8 of the William Styron collection housed in the Manuscript Department, Perkins Library, Duke University. References to early versions of *Lie Down in Darkness* are to this material.

4. See "Lie Down in Darkness," in *This Quiet Dust*, for Styron's own discussion of his use of ceremonials in this novel. In the manuscript of an article for *Le Figaro* (published May 7, 8, 1983), housed in Box 16 of the Styron collection at Duke University, Styron dis-

cusses the influence of film on his work. In reference to *Lie Down in Darkness* he writes, "So many scenes from that book were set up in my mind as I might have set them up as a director. My authorial eye became a camera, and the page became a set or sound stage upon which my characters entered or exited and spoke their lines as if from a script."

5. STYRON'S FAREWELL TO ARMS: WRITINGS ON THE MILITARY

1. Introduction to section called "The Service," *This Quiet Dust*, p. 190.
2. Introduction to the Norwegian edition of *The Long March*, in *This Quiet Dust*, p. 300.
3. "Marriott, the Marine," *Esquire*, 76 (September 1971), p. 103.
4. The revised typescript of *In the Clap Shack*, housed in Box 8 of Duke University's Styron collection, reveals that in this late stage of the writing, Styron changed many first-person pronouns to third-person in Glanz's speeches.
5. Styron was reading *Lieutenant Calley, His Own Story* at about the same time as he worked on *In the Clap Shack*. One handwritten notation about Calley's memoirs, housed in Box 16 of Duke's Styron collection, bears on Styron's play: "The *IRONY* (unconscious) of [Calley's] worry about BLOW-JOB[.] 'Because if a GI is getting a blow-job he isn't destroying Communism.' 'He isn't combat effective.' Loony, almost. GETTING HIS OPTIONS CONFUSED AS ALL PURITAN AMERICANS."
6. "Calley," *New York Times Book Review*, September 12, 1971, reprinted in *This Quiet Dust*, p. 225. The section of *This Quiet Dust* entitled "The Service" contains several of Styron's essays on war. Styron's remarks on fear of Communism are contained in his 1981 commencement address at Duke University; the manuscript is housed in the Archives and Manuscripts division of Duke's Perkins Library.

6. SPEAKING THE UNSPEAKABLE: *SOPHIE'S CHOICE*

1. William Styron, *Sophie's Choice* (New York: Random House, 1979), p. 198.
2. Styron defends his ornate vocabulary by stating that extraordinary

words keep the mind active (presumably the reader's as well as the writer's), and that he "would rather err in the usage of more ornate language than with language which has no vitality or color." Interview with Kevin Sack, p. 8.

3. This comical style is probably a holdover from the Yiddish literary tradition. We find it in authors ranging from Sholem Aleichem to Saul Bellow. Here is Bellow's *Herzog*, listening patiently to Ramona's philosophizing: "Much of what she said was perfectly right. She was a clever woman and, even better, a dear woman. She had a good heart. And she had on black lace underpants. He knew she did." (Greenwich: Fawcett Crest, 1965), p. 246. In Heller's *Good as Gold*, a description of Bruce Gold's schoolmate, Lieberman, relies on this style for its humor:

> "By the time Gold entered Abraham Lincoln High School, Lieberman was already there as a sophomore, having vaulted ahead one school year somehow, and was making a name for himself as an outstanding student and a *putz*. He was on the staff of the literary magazine and the school newspaper. By his junior year, Lieberman took uncontested control of both. He was active in political matters and co-captain of the debating team, which always lost. . . .To teach Gold his place, Lieberman mailed twenty-five of *his* poems to *The Saturday Review of Literature*. Thirty-nine came back.
> "What do I care?" Lieberman sneered. "When I grow up I'm gonna be rich. I'll be more famous than anyone. I'm gonna marry a rich and famous heiress. I'll never lose my hair. I'll wear lots of rings. I'll go into politics and win. I'll be a mayor, a senator, and the governor of all New York. I'll be a millionaire. When I grow up," he vowed, "I'm gonna fuck a girl."
> Instead, he went to college.

[Joseph Heller, *Good as Gold* (New York: Simon and Schuster, 1979, p. 63)]

4. Robert K. Morris, "Interviews with William Styron," in *The Achievement of William Styron*, ed. Robert K. Morris with Irving Malin, revised edition (Athens: University of Georgia Press, 1981), pp. 58–59.

5. *Ibid*, p. 67.

7. THE SEARCH FOR A MEANINGFUL THEME

1. These are collected in the scrapbooks kept by William Clark Styron, Sr., and are housed in the Manuscripts Department, Perkins Library, Duke University.

2. So he says in the PBS documentary, *William Styron: A Portrait* (1982), video cassette, Manuscripts Department, Perkins Library, Duke University. Styron's favorite strolling place near his home in Roxbury, Connecticut, is the nearby cemetery on the hill.
3. Michiko Kakutani, p. 26. Styron and his wife Rose both speak to this issue in *William Styron: A Portrait*.
4. "Interviews with William Styron," in *The Achievement of William Styron*, pp. 56–57.
5. William Styron, "My Generation," *Esquire*, 70 (October 1968), pp. 123–24.
6. CBS cable TV interview with Styron on "Signature," 1981. Video cassette in Perkins Library, Duke University.
7. Styron's remarks during "Lone Vigil '84," November 18, 1984.
8. "Interviews with William Styron," pp. 67–68.
9. *Ibid*, p. 69.
10. *Ibid*, p. 35.
11. John Kenny Crane, p. 5.
12. Kakutani, p. 3.
13. William Styron, "Letter to an Editor," *Paris Review*, 1 (Spring 1953), p. 13.
14. *Ibid*.
15. Molly Haskell, "Women in the Movies Grow Up," *Psychology Today*, January 1983, p. 26.
16. Robert Alter, "Styron's Stingo," *Saturday Review*, July 7, 1979, p. 43.
17. *Durham Morning Herald*, May 12, 1968, p. 6A.
18. Pierre Dommergues, "William Styron à Paris," *Le Monde*, April 26, 1974, p. 26. Quoted in Valarie M. Arms, p. 312. After publishing *The Confessions of Nat Turner*, Styron found in Georg Lukacs's *The Historical Novel* the full articulation of (and justification for) Styron's instincts about the relationship of the historical novelist to his material. "William Styron on Nat Turner," *The Bulletin of the Center for the Study of Southern Culture and Religion*, 2 (Summer 1978), p. 5.
19. William Styron, Acceptance Speech for the Howells Medal, reprinted in *Critical Essays on William Styron*, p. 226.
20. William Styron, "Hell Reconsidered," *New York Review of Books*, June 20, 1978, reprinted in *This Quiet Dust*, p. 103.
21. Flannery O'Connor, *The Habit of Being*, edited and with an introduction by Sally Fitzgerald (New York: Farrar Straus and Giroux, 1979), p. 498. For a concise history of Styron's critical reception in France see Valarie M. Arms.
22. Dommergues, p. 19.

23. Louis Rubin has done a good job of explaining the differences as he sees them between Faulkner's writing and Styron's in "Notes on a Southern Writer in Our Time," collected in *The Achievement of William Styron*, pp. 70–105.

AFTERWORD

1. Styron's notes for the novel, housed in Box 9 of Duke University's Perkins Library, Manuscripts Department, indicate the outrage he felt at the implication by talk-show host David Susskind that only Jews would be interested in discussing the Holocaust. Styron has made this same point in talk-show interviews of his own (Dick Cavett show, 1979) as well as in such essays as "Hell Reconsidered," reprinted in *This Quiet Dust*, p. 103.
2. Irving Saposnik, "Bellow, Malamud, Roth . . . . . . .and Styron? or One Jewish Writer's Response," *Judaism*, 31 (Summer 1982), pp. 322–32.
3. F. K. Frank. "The Presentment of the Jew in American Fiction," *Bookman*, 71 (1930), p. 274. Quoted in Sol Liptzin, *The Jew in American Literature* (New York: Bloch Publishing Co., 1966), pp. 153–54. For an oversimplified but vigorous view, see Leslie Fiedler in "Zion as Main Street," collected in *Waiting for the End* (New York: Stein and Day, 1964), pp. 65–88; and, for a full treatment of these issues, through the nineteenth century, Louis Harap's *The Image of the Jew in American Literature* (Philadelphia: The Jewish Publication Society of America, 1974).
4. Styron discusses his feelings toward the Jews in an interview with Raymond Sokolov conducted on September 28, 1967. An unedited typescript is housed in Box 7 of Duke's Styron collection. See "reel two," pp. 13–15. Portions of this interview were published in *Newsweek*, for 16 October 1967 (see below).
5. Sokolov, *Newsweek* article, p. 68.
6. Notes for *Inheritance of Night*, in which the Jew is called Sidney Harris rather than Harry Miller, are contained in Box 8 of Duke's Styron collection.
7. Unedited Sokolov interview, "reel one," pp. 50–51, 53–54; "reel two," p. 15.
8. The Jew in drama is explored by Ellen Schiff in *From Stereotype to Metaphor: The Jew in Contemporary Drama* (Albany: State University of New York Press, 1982). The book refers to Styron's play.

9. Unedited Sokolov interview, "reel one," p. 24.

10. Various versions of *In the Clap Shack* are collected in Box 8 of Duke's Styron collection.

11. Unedited Sokolov interview, "reel 2," pp. 15–16.

12. Sokolov, *Newsweek* article, p. 66.

13. According to William Styron's best recollection, personal correspondence, December 20, 1986.

14. Leslie Lapidus, of course. See Styron's comments in Kevin Sack, p. 8.

15. Unedited Sokolov interview, "reel one," p. 48.

16. Bellow's joking classification for himself and his colleagues, quoted by Leslie Field in "Saul Bellow and the Critics—After the Nobel Award," *Modern Fiction Studies*, 25 (1979–80), p. 5.

17. Philip Rahv, "The Editor Interviews William Styron," *Modern Occasions*, 1 (Fall 1971), p. 502. See Ruth R. Wisse, *The Schlemiehl as Modern Hero* (Chicago: University of Chicago Press, 1971).

18. So Styron has said in an interview with Dannye Romine, Book Editor for the *Charlotte Observer*, p. 5F, issue unknown.

19. See Percy's remarks in Lewis A. Lawson, "Walker Percy's Southern Stoic," *Southern Literary Journal*, 3 (Fall 1970), p. 10.

Selected Bibliography

These titles are culled from, and update, *William Styron: A Bibliography*, compiled by Jackson R. Bryer and published in *The Achievement of William Styron*, ed. Robert K. Morris (1981). For a more extensive listing of works by and about Styron, up until 1980, the reader is advised to consult that bibliography. An *annotated* selected bibliography of works about Styron and modern literature, until 1971, is found in Ratner (see below).

1. WORKS BY WILLIAM STYRON

Novels

Lie Down in Darkness. New York: Bobbs-Merrill, 1951.
The Long March. New York: Random House, Modern Library, 1956.
Set This House on Fire. New York: Random House, 1960.
The Confessions of Nat Turner. New York: Random House, 1967.
Sophie's Choice. New York: Random House, 1979.

Play and Screenplay

In the Clap Shack. New York: Random House, 1973.
"Dead!" *Esquire*, 80 (December 1973) [Screenplay by Styron and John Phillips].

Short Fiction

"Where the Spirit Is." *The Archive* (Duke University), 57 (January 1944).
"The Long Dark Road." *The Archive*, 57 (March 1944). Reprinted in *One and Twenty: Duke Narrative and Verse, 1924–1945*, selected by William Blackburn, Durham, N. C.: Duke University Press, 1945. And reprinted in *William Styron's "The Confessions of Nat Turner": A Critical Handbook*, ed. Friedman and Malin (see below).
"Sun on the River." *The Archive*, 58 (September 1944).
"A Story About Christmas." *The Archive*, 58 (December 1944).

"Autumn." *The Archive*, 58 (February 1945). Rpt. in *One and Twenty*.

"This is My Daughter." *The Archive*, 59 (May 1946).

"The Ducks." *The Archive*, 50 (October 1946).

"A Moment in Trieste." *American Vanguard*, ed. Don. M. Wolfe. Ithaca and New York: Cornell University Press, 1948.

"The Enormous Window." *1950 American Vanguard: A Collection of Short Stories*, ed. Charles I. Glicksberg. New York: Cambridge Publishing Company, 1950.

"Long March." *discovery*, 1 (February 1953).

"Marriott, the Marine." *Esquire*, 76 (September 1971).

"The Suicide Run." *American Poetry Review*, 3 (May/June 1974).

"Shadrach." *Esquire*, 90 (21 November 1978).

"Love Day." *Esquire*, 104 (August 1985).

Essays and Articles

"Letter to an Editor." *Paris Review*, 1 (Spring 1953), pp. 9–13.

"What's Wrong with the American Novel?" *American Scholar*, 24 (Autumn 1955), pp. 464–503. [Roundtable discussion with Ralph Ellison, Hiram Haydn, et al.]

"Introduction." *Best Short Stories from "The Paris Review."* New York: E. P. Dutton, 1959.

"Role of the Writer in America." *Michigan's Voices*, 2 (Spring 1962), pp. 7–10.

"Two Writers Talk It Over." *Esquire*, 60 (July 1963), pp. 57–59. [Discussion with James Jones.]

[Statement on Vietnam War]. *Authors Take Sides on Vietnam*, ed. Cecil Woolf and John Bagguley. London: Peter Owen, 1967.

"Violence in Literature." *American Scholar*, 37 (Summer 1968), pp. 482–96. [Roundtable discussion with Robert Penn Warren, Theodore Solotaroff, and Robert Coles.] Reprinted in *The Writer's World*, ed. Elizabeth Janeway. New York: McGraw Hill, 1969.

"My Generation." *Esquire*, 70 (October 1968), pp. 123–24. Reprinted in *"Esquire": The Best of Forty Years*. New York: David McKay, 1973.

"On Creativity." *Playboy*, 15 (December 1968), pp. 136–39.

"The Uses of History in Fiction." *Southern Literary Journal*, 1 (Spring 1969), pp. 57–90. [Discussion with Ralph Ellison, Robert Penn Warren, and C. Van Woodward.]

"Presentation to Thomas Pynchon of the Howells Medal for Fiction of the Academy." *Proceedings of The American Academy of Arts and Letters and the National Institute of Arts and Letters*, 2nd series, No. 26 (1976), pp. 43–46.

"An Indulgence of Authors' Self-Portraits." *Paris Review*, 17 (Fall 1976), p. 122. Reprinted in *Self-Portrait*: *Book People Picture Themselves*. New York: Random House, 1976.

[Statement about William Blackburn.] *Duke Encounters*, Durham, N. C.: Duke University Office of Publications, 1977.

"The South: Distance and Change: A Conversation with Robert Penn Warren, William Styron, and Louis D. Rubin," in *The American South*: *Portrait of a Culture*, ed. Louis D. Rubin. Baton Rouge: Louisiana State University Press, 1980.

"'Race Is The Plague of Civilization': An Author's View." *U. S. News & World Report*, 88 (28 January 1980), pp. 65–66.

"Almost a Rhodes Scholar: A Personal Reminiscence." *South Atlantic Bulletin*, 45 (May 1980), pp. 1–7.

"In Praise of Vineyard Haven." *New York Times Magazine*, 15 June 1980, p. 30. Reprinted in *On the Vineyard*, ed. Peter Simon. New York: Anchor Press/Doubleday, 1980.

"The Conversation: Candice Bergen & William Styron." *Esquire* (January 1982), pp. 86–93.

This Quiet Dust and Other Writings. New York: Random House, 1982.

2. WORKS ABOUT WILLIAM STYRON

Aldridge, John W. "The Society of Three Novels," in *In Search of Heresy*. New York: McGraw-Hill, 1956.

_____. "William Styron and the Derivative Imagination," in *Time to Murder and Create*: *The Contemporary Novel in Crisis*. New York: David McKay, 1966.

Arms, Valarie Meliotes. "An Interview with William Styron." *Contemporary Literature*, 20 (Winter 1979), pp. 1–12.

_____. "William Styron and the Spell of the South." *Mississippi Quarterly*, 34 (1980–81), pp. 25–36.

Atlas, James. "A Talk with William Styron." *New York Times Book Review*, May 27, 1979, pp. 1, 18.

Baker, John. "William Styron," in *Conversations with Writers, II*, ed. Matthew J. Bruccoli, C. E. Frazer Clark, Jr., Richard Layman, Margaret M. Duggan, Glenda G. Fedricci, and Clara L. White. Detroit: Gale, 1977. Vol. 3, pp. 257–82.

Brandriff, Welles T. "The Role of Order and Disorder in *The Long March*." *English Journal*, 56 (January 1967), pp. 54–59.

Brunaur, Dalma H. "Black and White: The Archetypal Myth and Its Development." *Barat Review*, 6 (Spring/Summer 1971), pp. 12–19.

Bryant, Jerry H. *The Open Decision: The Contemporary American Novel and Its Intellectual Background*. New York: Free Press, 1970.

Butterworth, Keen. "William Styron," in *Dictionary of Literary Biography*. Vol. 2. *American Novelists Since World War II*, ed. Jeffrey Helterman and Richard Layman. Detroit: Gale, 1978.

Caputo, Philip. "Styron's Choices." *Esquire*, 106 (December 1986), pp. 136–59.

Carver, Wayne. "The Grand Inquisitor's Long March." *Denver Quarterly*, 1 (Summer 1966), pp. 37–64.

Casciato, Arthur D., and James L. W. West III. *Critical Essays on William Styron*. Boston: G. K. Hall & Co., 1982.

Clarke, John Henrik, ed. *William Styron's ''Nat Turner'': Ten Black Writers Respond*. Boston: Beacon Press, 1968.

Cobbs, John L. "Baring the Unbearable: William Styron and the Problems of Pain." *Mississippi Quarterly*, 34 (1980–81), pp. 15–24.

Coles, Robert. "Arguments: The Turner Thesis." *Partisan Review*, 35 (Summer 1968), pp. 412–14.

Cooke, Michael. "Nat Turner: Another Response." *Yale Review*, 58 (Winter 1969), pp. 295–301.

Cowley, Malcolm. "American Novels Since the War." *New Republic*, 129 (28 December 1953), pp. 16–18.

Crane, John Kenny. *The Root of All Evil: The Thematic Unity of William Styron's Fiction*. Columbia, S. C.: University of South Carolina Press, 1984.

Davis, Robert Gorham. "Styron and the Students." *Critique*, 3 (Summer 1960), pp. 37–46.

Dempsey, David. "Talk with William Styron." *New York Times Book Review*, September 9, 1951, p. 27.

Doar, Harriet. "Interview with William Styron." *Red Clay Reader*, 1 (1964), pp. 26–30.

Duff, John B., and Peter M. Mitchell, eds. *The Nat Turner Rebellion: The Historical Event and the Modern Controversy*. New York: Harper & Row, 1971.

Duberman, Martin. "William Styron's *Nat Turner* and Ten Black Writers Respond," in *The Uncompleted Past*. New York: Random House, 1969.

Eggenschwiler, David. "Tragedy and Melodrama in *The Confessions of Nat Turner*." *Twentieth Century Literature*, 20 (January 1974), pp. 19–33.

Fielding, Andrew. "William Styron: An 'Unfamous' Great Writer Brings Out a New Novel, *Sophie's Choice*." *Horizon*, 22 (June 1979), pp. 60–67.

Fossum, Robert H. *William Styron*. Grand Rapids, Michigan: William B. Eerdmans, 1968.

Foster, Richard. "An Orgy of Commerce: William Styron's *Set This House on Fire*." *Critique*, 3 (Summer 1960), pp. 59–70.

Friedman, Melvin J. *William Styron*. Popular Writers Series, No. 3. Bowling Green, Ohio: Bowling Green University Popular Press, 1974.

_____ , and Irving Malin, eds. *William Styron's "The Confessions of Nat Turner": A Critical Handbook*. Belmont, Calif.: Wadsworth, 1970.

Galloway, David. "The Absurd Man as Tragic Hero" and "A William Styron Checklist," in *The Absurd Hero in American Fiction*, rev. ed. (Austin, Texas: University of Texas Press, 1970), pp. 51–81, 208–20.

Geismar, Maxwell. "William Styron: The End of Innocence," in *American Moderns: From Rebellion to Conformity*. New York: Hill and Wang, 1958.

Griffin, Jack, Jerry Homsy, and Gene Stelzig. "A Conversation with William Styron." *The Handle* (University of Pennsylvania), 2 (Spring 1965), pp. 16–29.

Gossett, Louise Y. "The Cost of Freedom: William Styron," in *Violence in Recent Southern Fiction*. Durham, N. C.: Duke University Press, 1965.

Halpern, Daniel. "Checking In with William Styron." *Esquire*, 78 (August 1972), pp. 142–43.

Hays, Peter L. "The Nature of Rebellion in *The Long March*." *Critique*, 8 (Winter 1965–1966), pp. 70–74.

Holder, Alan. "Styron's Slave: *The Confessions of Nat Turner*." *South Atlantic Quarterly*, 68 (Spring 1969), pp. 167–80.

Howard, Jane. "Rose Styron." *Vogue*, 151 (May 1968), pp. 184–89, 274–75.

Huffman, James R. "A Psychological Redefinition of William Styron's *Confessions of Nat Turner*." *Literary Review*, 24 (Winter 1981), pp. 279–307.

Kakutani, Michiko. "William Styron on His Life and Work," *New York Times Book Review*, December 12, 1982, pp. 3, 26.

Klotz, Marvin. "The Triumph Over Time: Narrative Form in William Faulkner and William Styron." *Mississippi Quarterly*, 17 (Winter 1963–1964), pp. 9–20.

Kort, Wesley A. "*The Confessions of Nat Turner* and the Dynamic of Revolution," in *Shriven Selves: Religious Problems in Recent American Fiction*. Philadelphia: Fortress Press, 1972.

Lang, John. "God's Averted Face: Styron's *Sophie's Choice*." *American Literature*, 55 (May 1983), pp. 215–32.

Lawson, John Howard. "William Styron: Darkness and Fire in the Modern Novel." *Mainstream*, 13 (October 1960), pp. 9–18.

Mackin, Cooper R. *William Styron*. Southern Writers Series, No. 7. Austin, Texas: Steck-Vaughn, 1969.

Mailer, Norman. "Norman Mailer vs. Nine Writers." *Esquire*, 60 (July 1963), pp. 63–69, 105.

Markos, Donald. "Margaret Whitehead in *The Confessions of Nat Turner.*" *Studies in the Novel*, 4 (Spring 1972), pp. 52–59.

Matthiessen, Peter, and George Plimpton. "William Styron," in *Writers at Work: The ''Paris Review'' Interviews*, ed. Malcolm Cowley. New York: Viking Press, 1959.

McNamara, Eugene. "William Styron's *Long March*: Absurdity and Authority." *Western Humanities Review*, 15 (Summer 1961), pp. 267–72.

Meeker, Richard K. "The Youngest Generation of Southern Fiction Writers," in *Southern Writers: Appraisals in Our Time*, ed. R. C. Simonini, Jr. Charlottesville: University of Virginia Press, 1961.

Mellard, James M. "This Unquiet Dust: The Problem of History in Styron's *The Confessions of Nat Turner.*" *Mississippi Quarterly*, 36 (Fall 1983), pp. 525–43.

Mellen, Joan. "Polemics—William Styron: The Absence of a Social Definition." *Novel*, 4 (Winter 1971), pp. 158–70.

Mills, Hilary. "Creators on Creating: William Styron." *Saturday Review* (September 1980), pp. 46–50.

Moore, L. Hugh. "Robert Penn Warren, William Styron, and the Use of Greek Myth." *Critique*, 8 (Winter 1965–1966), pp. 75–87.

Morris, Robert K., with Irving Malin, ed. *The Achievement of William Styron*. Rev. ed. Athens: University of Georgia Press, 1981.

Morse, J. Mitchell. "Social Relevance, Literary Judgment, and the New Right; or, The Inadvertent Confessions of William Styron." *College English*, 30 (May 1969), pp. 605–16.

Mudrick, Marvin. "Mailer and Styron" and "Postscript 1970," in *On Culture and Literature*. New York: Horizon Press, 1970.

O'Connell, Shaun. "Expense of Spirit: The Vision of William Styron." *Critique*, 8 (Winter 1965–1966), pp. 20–33.

———. "William Styron: In the Refracted Light of Reminiscence." *Boston Sunday Globe*, 27 April 1975, Magazine, pp. 30, 32–39.

O'Connor, William Van. "John Updike and William Styron: The Burden of Talent," in *Contemporary American Novelists*, ed. Harry T. Moore. Carbondale: Southern Illinois University Press, 1964.

Ownbey, Ray. "Discussions with William Styron." *Mississippi Quarterly*, 30 (Spring 1977), pp. 283–95.

Pearce, Richard. *William Styron*. University of Minnesota Pamphlets on

American Writers, No. 98. Minneapolis: University of Minnesota Press, 1971.

Perry, J. Douglas, Jr. "Gothic as Vortex: The Form of Horror in Capote, Faulkner, and Styron." *Modern Fiction Studies*, 19 (Summer 1973), pp. 153–67.

Phillips, John. "Styron Unlocked." *Vogue*, 150 (December 1967), pp. 216–17, 267–71, 278.

Poirier, Richard. "A Literature of Law and Order," in *The Performing Self*: *Compositions and Decompositions in the Language of Contemporary Life*. New York: Oxford University Press, 1971.

[Rahv, Philip]. "The Editor Interviews William Styron." *Modern Occasions*, 1 (Fall 1971), pp. 501–10.

Ratner, Marc L. *William Styron*. New York: Twayne Publishers, 1972.

Roth, Philip. "Writing American Fiction." *Commentary*, 31 (March 1961), pp. 223–33.

Rubenstein, Richard L. "The South Encounters the Holocaust: William Styron's *Sophie's Choice*." *Michigan Quarterly Review*, 20 (Fall 1981), pp. 425–42.

Ruderman, Judith, "Milton's Choices: Styron's Use of Robert Frost's Poetry in *Lie Down in Darkness*." *CLA Journal*, 27 (December 1983), pp. 141–51.

Sack, Kevin. "Duke's Choice," *Tobacco Road*, 4 (May 1981), pp. 6–8, 32.

Saposnik, Irving S. "Bellow, Malamud, Roth . . . . and Styron? Or One Jewish Writer's Response." *Judaism*, 31 (Summer 1982), pp. 322–32.

Scheick, William J. "Discarded Watermelon Rinds: The Rainbow Aesthetic of Styron's *Lie Down in Darkness*." *Modern Fiction Studies*, 24 (Summer 1978), pp. 247–54.

Schickel, Richard. "The Old Criticism and the New Novel." *Wisconsin Studies in Contemporary Literature*, 5 (Winter-Spring 1964), pp. 26–36.

Shapiro, Herbert. "*The Confessions of Nat Turner*: William Styron and His Critics." *Negro American Literature Forum*, 9 (Winter 1975), pp. 99–104.

Sitkoff, Harvard, and Michael Wreszin. "Whose Nat Turner: William Styron vs. the Black Intellectuals." *Midstream*, 14 (November 1968), pp. 10–20.

Sokolov, Raymond. "Into the Mind of Nat Turner," *Newsweek*, October 16, 1967, pp. 65–69.

Stanford, Mike. "An Interview with William Styron." *The Archive* (Duke University), 89 (Spring 1977), pp. 84–93.

Stevenson, David L. "Styron and the Fiction of the Fifties." *Critique*, 3

(Summer 1960), pp. 47–58.

Suter, Anthony. "Transcendence and Failure: William Styron's *Lie Down in Darkness.*" *Caliban 12* (Toulouse), 11 (1975), pp. 157–66.

Tragle, Henry Irving. "Styron and His Sources." *Massachusetts Review,* 11 (Winter 1970), pp. 134–53.

Urang, Gunnar. "The Broader Vision: William Styron's *Set This House on Fire.*" *Critique,* 8 (Winter 1965–1966), pp. 47–69.

———. "The Voices of Tragedy in the Novels of William Styron," in *Adversity and Grace: Studies in Recent American Literature,* ed. Nathan A. Scott, Jr. Chicago: University of Chicago Press, 1968.

Uya, Okon E. "Race, Ideology and Scholarship in the United States: William Styron's *Nat Turner* and Its Critics." *American Studies International,* 15 (Winter 1976), pp. 63–81.

Via, Dan O., Jr. "Law and Grace in Styron's *Set This House on Fire.*" *Journal of Religion,* 51 (April 1971), pp. 125–36.

Watkins, Floyd C. "*The Confessions of Nat Turner*: History and Imagination," in *In Time and Place: Some Origins of American Fiction.* Athens: University of Georgia Press, 1977.

West, James L. W. III. *William Styron: A Descriptive Bibliography.* Preface by William Styron. Boston: G. K. Hall, 1977.

———. "William Styron: A Biographical Account." *Mississippi Quarterly,* 34 (Winter 1980–81), pp. 2–7.

———, ed. *Conversations with William Styron.* Foreword by William Styron. Jackson: University Press of Mississippi, 1985.

———, and August J. Nigro. "William Blackburn and His Pupils: A Conversation." *Mississippi Quarterly,* 31 (Fall 1978), pp. 605–14.

White, John. "The Novelist as Historian: William Styron and American Negro Slavery." *Journal of American Studies,* 4 (February 1971), pp. 233–45.

Williams, Ernest P. "William Styron and His Ten Black Critics: A Belated Meditation." *Phylon,* 37 (June 1976), pp. 189–95.

Index

الأول ۱۹۱۳ ـ ۱۵